Cold Feet

a woman's guide to life

Jonathan Rice
Based on the scripts
by Mike Bullen

GRANADA
MEDIA

Based on the scripts by Mike Bullen.
Cold Feet is devised and written by Mike Bullen.

First published in Great Britain in 1999
by Granada Media an imprint of André Deutsch Limited

76 Dean Street
London W1V 5HA
www.vci.co.uk

in association with Granada Media Group
Text and Photographs Copyright ©Granada Media Group Ltd
1999

A catalogue record for this book is available from the British
Library.

ISBN 0 233 99732 6
Design by Essential Books

Printed and bound in the UK by Butler and Tanner Ltd,
Frome and London

10 9 8 7 6 5 4 3 2 1

Cold Fëët

Contents

I'm Rachel. Bradley.

Actually, I'm Rachel Louise Bumstead. I married Kris. Kris Bumstead. When we were students together at Manchester University (I read French).

In name only. Married, that is, not students. Pity the name was Bumstead.

No one knows. Or knew. Well, except Kris. It was a long time ago. It lasted twenty-three days and then he slept with my best friend, Suzy. They went off to India together to live in an ashram. So we never quite got round to the divorce.

I'm in advertising.

That's what a degree in French leads naturally into. I've been involved as account manager with lots of pretty successful campaigns. Things like, you know, "Wyatt's Jammy Mouthfuls, so yummy they fill your — oi, oi — tummy." And the ad with the skateboarding nun. And so on. It keeps the bank manager happy, at least.

Before I went into advertising, I had a season as a chalet girl in the French Alps. Now there I did use my French sometimes, although most of the holidaymakers we worked with were English, and after a hard day's skiing and partying, they spoke no language known to man. That was when I met Karen, my best friend. Karen came back to Manchester and within a few months had married David. He's funny. Funny peculiar rather than funny ha-ha, but funny nice as well. Not what I would have thought Karen would have married.

But then Kris is not what I thought I would have married.

If there's a man in my life now, it's Adam. He's completely irresponsible half of the time, and such an old fart the rest of the time. You'd think he was born middle-aged. What's a 28-year-old to do with a man who's 31 going on 50?

He'd be Cardigan Man except he doesn't have a cardie.

One day I'll buy him one.

Sex ought to be very simple, but somehow it never is. I don't mean technically. Technically it's not that difficult unless Adam is in one of his more imaginative moods, but emotionally it sometimes gets complicated. I mean, why did I get married to Kris when we were students, and why didn't I tell Adam about him all those years later? And then why, when I agreed to get a divorce, did I have sex with Kris (all quite legal, of course) when I should have been organising the paperwork for the decree? It all gets very messy, and not only when Adam is playing with custard.

IMPOTENCE

No, not a problem with my men. Sometimes I wish it was. If only Kris and Adam weren't both so bloody potent, and I hadn't got so drunk that night I met Kris to ask for a divorce, then I might never have had to leave Manchester behind.

Maybe I should never have said to Adam, "That's the last time I ever play Scrabble with you." Girls don't get pregnant playing Scrabble. Or not very often, anyway. But don't ever trust yourself to play strip Scrabble with Adam. I lost my bra to "snark".

RACHEL ON MUSIC

My favourite music? It changes all the time. The only consistency is my intense dislike of anything by Wet Wet Wet.

I have to put up with a lot of R.E.M. from Adam, and that man Morrissey. What is it about his voice that appeals to men who don't ever grow up?

What about Faithless? Not to be confused with Faith No More. Or Faith Hill. "Reverence" and "Sunday 8pm" are both great CDs. "God Is A DJ" and "Insomnia" are just beautiful music.

Then there's **Morcheeba.** I love their "Big Calm" album. I saw them performing a few years ago in a pub in deepest Kent, Sandwich or somewhere, before they ever had a record contract. They were great, even then.

RACHEL ON FILMS

I love films. It's a great passion. I go all the time. I like the old films, the classics like Kurosawa's "Seven Samurai" or anything by Ingmar Bergman. Actually, Ingmar Bergman only works when Adam is not there with me. But I like modern films too. Except "Four Weddings And A Funeral" because of that dreadful Wet Wet Wet song.

My favourite film?

"All About Eve". Best Picture Oscar for 1950, and quite possibly the best film of all time. As the posters said, "It's all about women…and their men." When one of the women is Bette Davis and one of the men is George Sanders, and the cast also includes Marilyn Monroe in one of her earliest screen roles, then it's bound to be a masterpiece. "Fasten your seat belts. It's going to be a bumpy ride", as Margo Channing (Bette Davis) says. **I love a bumpy ride.**

"King Of Comedy", there's another great film. And "Jean De Florette". And Charles Laughton's "Mutiny On The Bounty", and "In The Heat Of The Night" and "Gigi" and "Battleship Potemkin". There's a hundred wonder-ful films I could list, and all of them could be my favourite according to my mood. Or second favourite,

AGE

I've never really worried about age. Most of my men have been the standard age, say up to a couple of years older than me, but there was Danny at the office who is seven years younger, and Adam's teacher Mr. Chacksfield, who must be fifteen years older than me. He was a nice guy, but when he asked me out for dinner and I saw him sitting in the restaurant waiting for me, I realised that he was an old man. I mean, Adam is Cardigan Man, but it's only his clothes that are wrinkled, not his face.

Adam thinks I'm odd. I have dinner with somebody who he calls pre-pubescent, and then with somebody who he thinks is due his bus pass. He even had the nerve to suggest I was trying to do all seven ages of man. Well, you never know. I might.

WORK

I'm in advertising. Account manager. Advertising has a faster turnover than football management, so I've moved about a bit. When I joined my latest agency, Terry – he's the guy I report to, I've worked with him before – said he'd lost five staff that month. Three to competitors, one was pregnant, one'd had a break-down and one had gone travelling "to find himself".

"That's six. You said you'd lost five staff." I like to impress at an inter-view with my grasp of figures.

"No. The pregnant one went to a competitor. They don't know yet."

I report to Terry and Danny reports to me. Danny's only 21. It all works very well, because we are all good at our jobs. It's a very informal office. **There's only one rule. Workmates Don't Shag.** Not that Terry has ever had much time for it. The rule, that is, not the shagging.

Adam doesn't like Danny. When he stumbled across us having din-ner together, he made his feelings clear. To be exact, he said that his balls haven't dropped yet.

"You mean he's young."

"Young! He ordered off the junior menu. The wine waiter asked him for ID."

SONGS

I've only ever had two songs dedicated to me – unless you count Adam's repeated playing of "D-I-V-O-R-C-E" by Tammy Wynette while Kris was staying. One was written by Kris and one by Adam. They were both rather sweet.

Kris wrote:

SONG FOR RACHEL

O.K., so it doesn't rhyme or scan or anything, but when he played his guitar and sang it, it sounded really good.

You only get one chance in life
Well, I didn't make it known
You only get one chance at love
Well I didn't make it yeah.
If I could know exactly what I'd say to you tonight
If I could I wouldn't let you walk away
Come what may...

Adam wrote:

THE BALLAD OF RACHEL BRADLEY by Adam Williams

There was a girl called Rachel Bradley
Whose boyfriend loved her truly, deeply, madly
She was married to Kris with a K
But now that bollocks with a B has gone away
So Rachel's now a divorcee
Living with Adam in Didsbury
And Kris with a K, he's now her ex
So Rachel with an R, can we have some...

I finished it off for him.

Cold Feet

Adam isn't very good at romance. He's not a Clark Gable or a Paul Newman. He's not even a Humphrey Bogart or a strong, silent Toshiro Mifune — you know, the star of "The Seven Samurai". Adam, romantic soul that he is, would probably know Mifune as a star of "Grand Prix", that dreadful 60s film with James Garner among others.

And his small talk is not much to write home about either (not that I write home about anything very often). Words of love are not his strong points.

"I love you more than there are grains of sand on a beach," he told me the other night.

"You've used that one already."

"Flies around shite?"

You see what I mean. Where is the romance in that?

"As much as I love George Best."

OK, still not romantic, but definitely from the heart.

"Well, almost."

Runner-up to George Best. What more can a girl ask?

HOUSEHUNTING

Finding somewhere to live in Manchester is not very easy. Finding somewhere to live in Manchester with Adam is mission impossible.

For a start, the newspaper small ads never tell the full story.

"Ainsworth Street, handy for visits" means next door to Strangeways.

"East Road, good transport links" means the end of the runway at Manchester Airport.

"Pembroke Street". A prime location. "Single woman wanted to share large bedroom. Phone Martin". I think not.

And once you go out looking for a place, the estate agents are hardly any help.

"You're wise to rent, not buy. It's simpler when you split up."

"By process of elimination, this must be the lounge. I have no idea which way the garden faces – south, I think. Not that it makes any difference in Manchester."

It's amazing that anybody finds anywhere to live. Our house is in the middle of our road. Shakespeare Road, Didsbury.

Cold Fëĕt

ADAM'S ANNOYING LITTLE HABITS:
A long list

1. He can't even eat a peanut without it almost hitting the ceiling first.

2. He leaves things in the fridge for months.

3. He likes "The Sweeney" even though he reckons Dennis Waterman should have been arrested for that haircut.

4. He gets words like "teredo" when we are playing Scrabble and

5. He knows whether it means a) a piece of music which sounds the same when played backwards, or b) a doughy bread baked by the tribespeople of Papua New Guinea, or c) a marine mollusc that bores into and destroys submerged timber. (It's c)

6. He is such an old fart.

7. He was born middle-aged.

8. He nags. "Turn the music down!:" "Where'd you leave the car?" "Did you lock it?"

9. Just because I was stoned. What's wrong with a few joints now and again?

Those underpants are an annoying habit, in the original sense of the word "habit" — meaning "clothing", as Adam would be able to point out to all those who sit at a Scrabble board with him. I suspect he was deliberately trying to lose our game of Open Air Strip Scrabble at the time.

MARRIAGE

Been there. Done that. Then Adam asked me. But what's the point? Tax? Presents? To make a statement to the rest of the world? But is the rest of the world that interested?

If we have problems, it's because we've allowed things to become mundane. I don't want to risk that happening. And there's a danger that marriage can do that. I mean, when you see a married couple in their fifties, what do you think? That they're making do. But if they haven't made that commitment but are still together after all that time, then, as Adam says, they must have great sex.

And what's commitment? You use the same word for a relationship and a lunatic asylum. Not surprising, I suppose.

And then there's the cost. How much would a wedding cost? Five thousand pounds? Plus the honeymoon. All we could afford would be a few days in Devon. So why not blow the budget on a fortnight in Bali, and see if the mood takes us while we're there?

So who makes the best Formula 1 racing cars?

Bread - whole-meal
Pasta
Washing up liquid
Lampshade for bedside lamp
Captain Corelli's Mandolin
Tights
Try to find shoes
Milk
Loo paper
Underpants - Adam
Check - when is Jenny's
birthday - flowers?

TELEPHONES

Telephones are dangerous things. It took me a couple of weeks to decide to make the telephone call to Adam after we had bumped into each other in the supermarket car park. I might have known that he would lose my phone number. If I hadn't made that call, life would have been very different. Not better, just different.

Fantasies

Everybody has fantasies, Adam more than most. I mean, it's one thing for me to fantasise about making love in a shop window, but it's quite another thing to do it. That didn't stop Adam. And the shop window didn't stop the joyrider who came straight through the plate glass. Very embarrassing. Adam seems to live through his and everybody else's fantasies.

Maybe it's a male thing. You can almost hear Adam's brain clicking into wishful thinking mode, but Karen and Jenny say their men are just as unreal. He's lived his future six or seven times already, before he gets there in reality. He says it's fun, and much more interesting than analysing systems in Manchester all day. Like most men, he must have scored the winning goal in the World Cup Final a hundred times, and won the Lottery and several Oscars, but that's not all. He's imagined every sort of future for us, together and apart, and can tell from what he considers to be personal experience what is best for us. Now, I don't necessarily disagree with his conclusions, but I want to experience them at the same time as him, and not be told all the time that it was better (or sometimes worse) in his fantasies.

If you live in your dreams all the time, reality creeps past you without you noticing.

Those underpants — I'm sorry to keep returning to them but their image is burned across my memory — do not crop up often in my fantasies. I only wish they would crop up more often in Adam's washing machine.

MAGAZINE PERSONALITY QUIZZES

JUST SAY NO. They don't work and they only make you think that the man you are with is the wrong one, simply because it looks as though they are the right one. If you see what I mean. The answers all come out that he is the one for you, but you know he isn't.

1. "Is sex something you're
a) keen to avoid ❑   b) willing to suffer ❑
  c) gagging for more of?" ❑

Yes, the answer is c, but that's me, not him. Three points for me.

2. "In the morning does your boyfriend give you
a) flowers ❑   b) the post ❑
c) another orgasm?" ❑

The answer is all three, so I get six points.

3. "Does he contact you during the daytime
a) by Interflora ❑   b) by erotic e-mail ❑
c) by a drunken phone call on his mobile
from the pub?" ❑

What about by Mexican troubadour from a scissor lift? How many points do I get for that?

DIFFERENCES BETWEEN MANCHESTER AND LONDON

1. THE PAY. You earn more in London.

2. THE THEATRE. It's much better in London.

3. FLATS. OK so the rent is higher, but the choice is much better in London. And the views.

4. THE WEATHER. That goes without saying. You want a tan, live in London. You want a rust, live in Manchester.

5. MY FRIENDS. You want to live alone, live in London. You want a social life, live in Manchester.

6. ADAM. He's in Manchester. There's only Kris in London.

David's brother,

Can two people with identical genetic backgrounds be this different? For a start Nick's eight years younger. And he votes Labour. Always has. And he likes Massive Attack, Irvine Welsh and backpacking.

He took me to the theatre one night, which Jenny says proves he does share some tastes with David.

The play was not really David's taste, though. It was what they call "an intense social drama" with men beating women and taking their trousers down with a shout of "You bitch, you whore! You screw me, I'll screw you. You slag!"

God, it was brilliant. I don't think I drew breath for two hours.

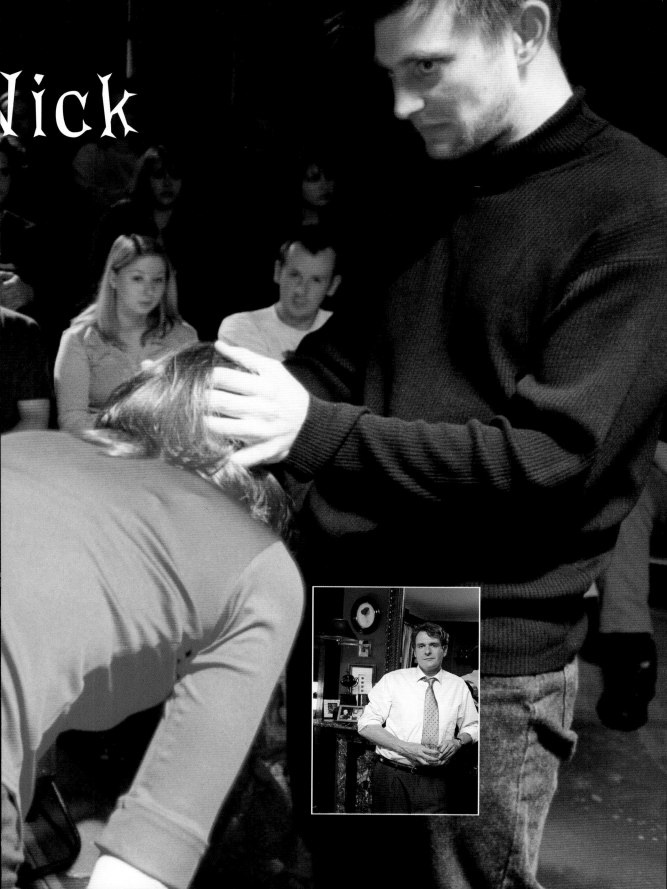

Nick

HOLIDAYS

When you live in Manchester, you need a holiday now and again. Before I climbed onto the treadmill of work (if you can call advertising "work" — everybody tells me it's just free lunches and gay artistic directors, but I haven't had much of the former and none of the latter have had me) I used to shove a couple of T-shirts, the latest P.D. James and some deodorant into my backpack and head off whenever and wherever I felt like it, but these days a holiday requires more planning.

Who to go with? After years of being too young to go anywhere on my own, I'm now too old to admit I'm on my own. Karen and I were chalet girls together years back, but that wasn't a holiday. These days she goes jetting off to Tuscany or Morocco with David, and I'd just be in the way. Adam would not want to go too far from a regular supply of beer and football, which means Ibiza or Benidorm. Or Manchester.

"It's oh so nice to go travelling, but it's so much nicer, yes it's so much nicer to come home", as a wise man with blue eyes and a very obvious wig
once sang. What did he know about anything?

Cold Fëet

WOMEN'S HEALTH

You've got to keep fit. I tried jogging with Emma next door, but she's only eighteen and I couldn't keep up after the first corner. Karen and I sometimes go to the gym together. You can run on the tread-mill there and nobody knows whether you are keeping up or not.

Karen's very aware of her health. She might smoke the occasional joint, but that's no more harmful than a glass of wine. **So I'm told.**

Jenny likes a glass of wine now and again. And vodka. And gin and tonics. But married to Pete and in charge of baby Adam, who wouldn't? Baby Adam's adorable, of course, but very hard work. Just like his godfather.

Famous

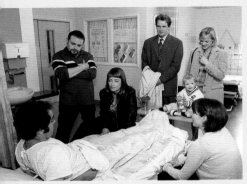

I'm not sure how the subject came up. Famous men whom Adam would describe as "monotesticulate".

Pete started it by saying, **"I bet there have been loads of famous people who only had one ball."**

"You mean, apart from Hitler?" Adam came up with one name straight away.

Pete, the trivia freak, was not so certain.

"Yeah. Well, Hitler is the most famous. And to be honest, I'm not even sure he did. I think they were just trying to ridicule him."

"Bruce Lee only had one." I read that somewhere, I'm sure.

"And he lived a full and active life," added Jenny.

"Till his death at the age of 32." Adam manages to put a downer on everything.

We couldn't think of anybody else. It's not the sort of thing you put on your cv, is it?

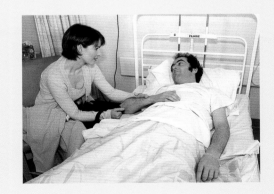

Cold Feet

FRAGILE

men

— with only one ball

One ball, maybe, but two enemas, three hours under the anaesthetics, four nurses attending to his every need, five visitors to his bedside, and a sixpack of beer courtesy of Pete. What more could a man want? And it was the first time I ever saw Adam in bed with clean sheets.

Don't say a word. Just listen. We love each other. We always have done. We always will. Regardless of what we do to each other. And God knows...

Love's about power. You love someone, you give them the power to hurt you, and inevitably they do.

"We have to talk". The worst four words in the English language. They mean "Goodbye forever. I'm moving on."

You make your own timing. You only miss the moment if you don't seize it. Because you're scared of what might happen if you do.

Friends are important, aren't they? They're the people you want to spend time with.

You can tell within the first ten seconds of meeting someone whether there's anything there.

Jenny Gifford

Cold Fëët

I'm Jenny. I'm Pete's wife. I'm baby Adam's Mum. That's not much of an introduction. There must be more to life than that.

Rachel has a good job in advertising. Karen edits books by that man who wrote "Blanket Of Tears". You know, the book with the bit where she's ironing. All I did was work in Personnel at the insurance company where Pete works. Well, I got to know the personnel. Or one of them at least.

Now I'm just a housewife and I don't even seem to have the nesting instinct. I love my baby, Adam, even if he does keep us awake at night. We wouldn't be without him for the world. But I don't take naturally to this motherhood thing. And I certainly don't take naturally to keeping the house clean.

I love my other baby, Pete. He's an annoying little habit, but I'm addicted to him. He takes naturally to making the house a tip, with empty beer cans and old newspapers and TV remotes and his mate Adam strewn all over the place. He says I should be pleased that he feels able to live entirely naturally at home, without having to make an effort to be anything different, and I suppose he has a point there — well, half a point — but wouldn't it be wonderful if his natural state included the inclination to put things into wastepaper baskets from time to time, or back in the fridge or in the washing machine?

There must be more to life than this.

Pete's Mum is quite the opposite. She's a cleanaholic. She thinks I'm a bit excitable, but that's only because I held a knife to her throat. Nobody could blame me for that. She was offering to hoover the carpets throughout yet again. Carpets can't stand more than one going over a week. Ten to fifteen sucks a week is just unnatural.

The only thing that worries me is that she says that all men marry their mothers. Surely I'll never be the one who causes Tesco to send out for extra supplies of "Mr. Muscle"?

JENNY ON FILMS

The last film I saw had Kevin Costner in it. It was all right. These days we just stay in, eat crap and watch TV.

I'm a sucker for romantic films. We've been to the cinema a couple of times with Rachel and Adam, but it's not much fun. Rachel only likes films in black and white and in obscure foreign languages like Japanese or Albanian, and Adam nicks all of Pete's popcorn. So they fight like two ten-year-olds while Rachel tries to explain the plot to me. It always involves honest but poor workers in an industrial wasteland, and you can generally expect the occasional crippled child in a wheelchair to roll into shot. And a bitter old lady who lost her only true love to a sniper's bullet on the Somme in 1916. Hardly laugh a minute.

I like "Sleepless in Seattle". Tom Hanks, Meg Ryan, a happy ending and a box of Kleenex. "Sleepless in Manchester" knows exactly how they feel.

JENNY ON MUSIC

Music? I don't really have much time to listen to music. Baby Adam tends to drown out all extraneous noise when he's awake, and when he's asleep we daren't put on any records in case we wake him up.

But I suppose it would be Mariah Carey. I love her version of "Without You". Or Celine Dion. That "Titanic" film was a bit ridiculous when you think about it, but the song was wonderful. When Celine hits a note, it stays hit. Like when I hit Pete.

SHOPPING LISTS

I don't use shopping lists. It just wastes time, and anyway, how do I know what they've got on special offer down at the supermarket? I just put Adam in the baby seat on the trolley and wander up and down the aisles pulling armfuls of stuff off the shelves as I go. Once I've filled the trolley, it's time to check out and go home. I always buy baby wipes, of course.

And instant lasagna and chips. And pizzas. And baked beans by the boxload.

BABY ALARMS

You can never have enough baby alarms, because you never know which room you are going to be in, and which room Adam is going to be in. I've even got one that according to the box it came in is "stylishly designed and you can use it abroad". Must have a hell of a long lead if you can use it abroad. I think generally, we wouldn't leave baby at home if we go overseas, so that particular feature of the baby alarm is unlikely to come into use. But it was recommended by "What Baby?" magazine.

MOBILE PHONES

Pete bought a mobile phone for when the baby was due. He wanted to keep the number exclusively for me to call him when I wanted to go to hospital, so that there'd be no chance of a cock-up. Well, if he hadn't lent it to Adam all might have been well, but that's another story.

Now everybody has our mobile phone number, which I suppose is logical. Adam and Rachel, and Jenny and David, and even Amy - the mad sex-hungry Amy at Pete's office - has the number. Pete's Mum rang Pete on it at the Tiddler's christening to tell him about his Dad's heart attack. Phone calls in church are never good news. It meant that the Tiddler had to have his Grandad's Algernon added to his name after all. Poor little sod, having to go through life with that extra burden. Reminds me of that old song, "A Boy Named Sue".

We still don't seem to get many calls on it recently, but maybe that's because Pete uses it most of the time, and perhaps he doesn't tell me about all the calls he makes. Couples aren't supposed to have secrets from each other.

APOLOGIES

I'll say sorry to anybody if it's my fault. I apologised to David for embarrassing him at that dreadful charity do, and I seem to have to apologise for Pete and baby Adam all the time. But I don't apologise to women with their sense of humour stuck up their arses, especially ones who call Pete a moron with a chromosome missing. I'm allowed to call Pete a moron, with or without a chromosome missing, but nobody else is. She should apologise to me.

I'll pay for the dress that got put out along with the table fire, but I won't apologise to the stupid cow.

The Sex Lives of Others

All couples have secrets from each other

Cold Fëët

Sometimes I think I know more about the sex lives of my friends than I do about my own. Not that there's a lot to know about my own.

Helping Adam to find a partner through the "Meeting Place" column of the Manchester Evening News was hard work, but somebody had to do it. Once I had persuaded Adam it was not called "Lonely Hearts", nor even "Sad Twats' Corner", he came round to my way of thinking.

Working with a dyslexic doesn't help. "Slim attractive virgin", I don't think so. "Slim attractive Virgoan" was what she was, "26" (which used to be a nice age), "seeks Taurean with a GSOH." Adam complained that he didn't have any GSOH's although he had several GCSEs. GSOH means "good sense of humour" – they always use that abbreviation in these columns. Or so I'm led to believe.

His reply began, "Dear Box R238 (that was my mother's name)". He said that demonstrated his GSOH. I said it made him sound like Norman Bates.

JENNIFER'S DIARY

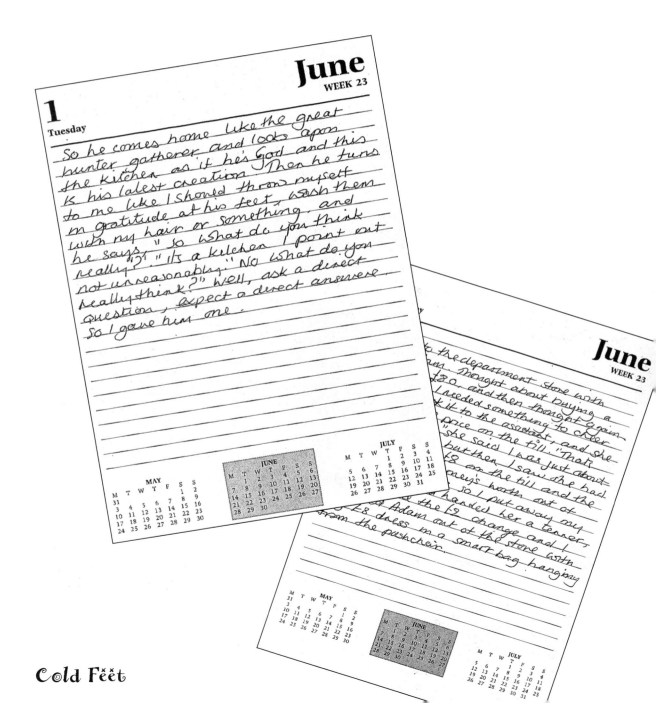

June
WEEK 23

1
Tuesday

So he comes home like the great hunter gatherer and looks upon the kitchen as if he's God and this is his latest creation. Then he turns to me like I should throw myself in gratitude at his feet, wash them with my hair or something, and he says, "So what do you think really?" "It's a kitchen," I point out not unreasonably. "No what do you really think?" Well, ask a direct question, expect a direct answer. So I gave him one.

June
WEEK 23

...to the department store with... ...um. Thought about buying a... ...£80 and then thought again... ...I needed something to cheer... ...it to the assistant, and she... ...price on the till. "That's... ..." she said. I was just about... ...but then I saw she had... ...£8 on the till and the... ...ney's worth out of... ...so I put away my... ...handed her a tenner, ...the £9 change and I ...an out of the store with ...£8 dress in a smart bag hanging from the pushchair.

ON KEEPING A DIARY

It's a good thing and a bad thing. It's a good thing if you can release your frustrations by writing them all down. It's a friend to talk to, and God knows I need a few friends to talk to sometimes.

But it's a bad thing if Pete reads it. A very bad thing. He might read things he doesn't want to know. That I don't want him to know.

The best place to keep a diary is under the mattress. Pete is hardly the Princess and the Pea. You could stick a herd of randy elephants under the mattress and after he's been down the pub with Adam, he wouldn't notice a thing. He'd sleep through it all like a baby. Well, any baby except the Tiddler, who doesn't do sleeping.

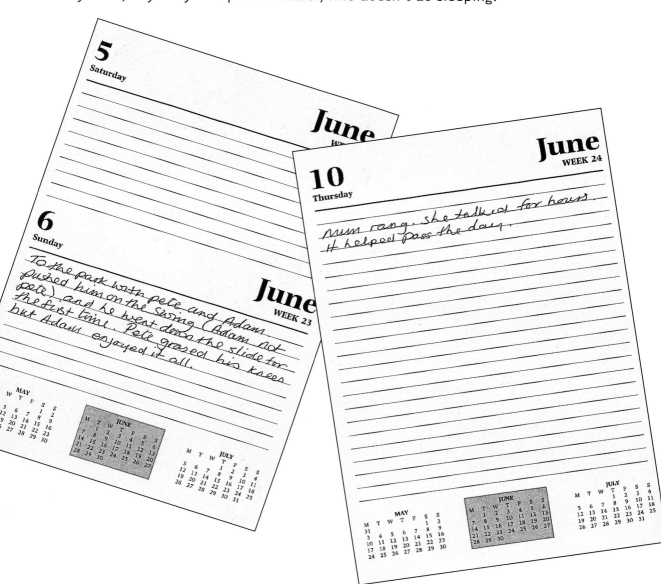

5 Saturday

June WEEK

6 Sunday

To the park with pete and Adam. pushed him on the swing (Adam not pete) and he went down the slide for the first time. Pete grazed his knees but Adam enjoyed it all.

June WEEK 23

10 Thursday

June WEEK 24

mum rang. she talked for hours. It helped pass the day.

AGƐ

Everything changes all the time. Pete's and my relationship has changed. And I think that sex will go on changing, every year until we're seventy. I doubt there'll be much movement involved by then, but it will still be us.

I sometimes see me and Pete as pensioners, living in an old people's home. Separate rooms, mind. We'd have chairs next to each other in the lounge and we'd sit, huddled together, complaining about nurses and how the Tiddler's too busy to visit his old folks. Except we wouldn't call him the Tiddler by then.

Somehow I can't always get that picture in my mind anymore. That'll be the Alzheimer's kicking in.

What's a kiss? When you find your mout is full of someone else's, that's a kiss

SISTERS

I have a sister, Sheila. She has several uses. She is Adam's godmother. Her being a Christian meant we were taking a bit of a risk in appointing her, and Pete was worried that when she said she'd like to do a reading from the Bible, she'd read the whole thing, Apocrypha and all, but we just about got away with it.

"If your hand causes you to sin, cut it off. It is better for you to enter life maimed than with two hands to go to hell to the unquenchable fire. And if your eye causes you to sin, pluck it out. It is better for you to enter the kingdom of god with one eye than with two eyes to be thrown into hell." Rousing stuff for a newborn babe to listen to. St. Matthew certainly knew how to tell a bedtime story.

She is also a great babysitter, apart from the bedtime stories. Her greatness is mainly based on the fact that she is a viable alternative to Adam, who is not a great babysitter. A keen babysitter, but not a great one.

COOKING

I don't like cooking. I don't like shopping for the ingredients, I don't like looking up the recipe in bloody Delia Smith, and I don't like the washing up that goes with any major cooking project. But I like watching baby Adam grow, and he'll only do that if I feed him. Pete and I can make do with takeaways.

None of my recipes include rocket, or basil or blueberries. Most of them include flour, sausages and curry powder.

The only time I cook in a big way is when Pete's Mum comes to stay, which thankfully is a very rare event. And even that horrendous prospect has its advantages. She just loves washing up, so I can make all the mess I like when I baste the chicken or bake a spotted dick. Pete's Mum will clear up behind me.

All the same, I don't like cooking. Unless you cook with wine.

I'm that used to takeaways I'd forgotten poppadoms could be warm.

Cold Fëët

Never go caravanning with Pete and his parents. I don't care how broke you are or how beautiful the North Cornwall coast can be in September. Believe me, it's not worth it. Pete and his Dad argued all the way over the best route, and which low bridges to avoid and where to stop for petrol, lunch and several pees. Pete's Mum wanted to stop the car at every opportunity to empty the ashtrays, which I had thoughtlessly filled with sweet wrappers. And when I volunteered to ride in the caravan, I was told in no uncertain terms by all three of them that it is illegal. Driving a woman insane is legal, apparently, but riding in a moving caravan is punishable by death. Give me the punishment any day.

Fantasies

I'm a simple hard working Victorian maid performing my daily chores, when the firm but fair hand of my Master pins me to the parquet.

"You're a whore, damn it, but I love you!"

"Quiet, Mistress might hear."

Or something like that...

It must be a terrible thing, to be with one person and in love with another.

KEEPING SECRETS

Rachel and Adam have an odd relationship, although it may not be as odd as the relationship between Pete and Adam. They know everything about each other, or so it seems, but only tell each other the unimportant things. And then they tell each other not to tell anybody else. And they think they won't. Tell anybody else, that is.

But who could ever keep a secret? Not me, that's for sure.

So, for example, Adam is surprised when Rachel finds out he's in hospital, and can't believe it's her when he comes round from the anaesthetic.

"The only people I've told are Pete and Jenny, and I told them not to tell anyone. So quid pro quo, you don't know."

"Unless they felt that with something as important as this, they owed it to you to break their promise and tell the people closest to you."

Actually, even if it had been unimportant, we might well have broken our promise. A secret's no fun unless you can tell somebody else. Then it's not a secret any more.

Cold Feet

Holidays are best on a beach. A beach in the north-east in the middle of winter may not quite be Cephalonia in June, but a friend's a friend and there's not much you can't do on the sand if you've got a mac and a stout pair of wellies on even on the coldest day of the year. That's the Tiddler's philosophy, anyway, and I'll go along with whatever he wants. No choice really.

PROCREATION

Procreation is fun. It's not the whole point of marriage maybe, but it sure beats dusting and shopping and being polite to the in-laws. Pete may not be what Rachel calls "sex on legs", but he is POTENT. We had to put in a great deal of practice before we felt we were ready for embarking on the Tiddler, but once we decided to go for it, all those dark nights of rehearsal paid off. I was pregnant within days.

The only thing we got wrong was the sex. The gender, I mean. The baby is a boy, and I wanted a girl. **So we will just have to practise some more.**

Cold Fèèt

CHILDBIRTH

Never again. The books never prepare you for what it's actually like. Mind you, I never got to read the books during pregnancy, because Pete was reading them all the time. More than reading them, really. More like learning them off by heart, like a Shakespeare play before the GCSE. But they never really tell you about the pain.

Women have been giving birth for quite some time, so there's nothing very new about it. They have whole columns devoted to it every day in the posh newspapers. But for me, it was the first time, and I think it better be the last as well. **I mean it HURTS.** It really hurts.

I should have guessed the baby would be a boy and not the girl we were expecting. Only a bloke could cause a woman so much pain. But the first time I looked at him, I forgave him.

The Tiddler, that is. I'm not sure I'll ever forgive Pete.

THE TIDDLER

When Baby Adam was born, we weren't expecting him. Well, of course we were expecting a baby, but we weren't expecting *him*. We were expecting a her, not a him. We didn't even have a name for a boy. Pete suggested Louis (he was singing "What A Wonderful World" to himself in that tuneless voice of his at the time), and also Felix – we don't even have a cat – but I just knew we wouldn't need a boy's name.

So the Tiddler was a shock. He ended up Adam Preston Algernon, named after his godfather, the motorcycle cop and his grandfather in that order. If Pete hadn't given his mobile to Adam in a drunken moment the night before, it is quite likely that the baby would just have been called Algernon, because we wouldn't have needed a motorcycle cop to get Pete to the hospital, and Adam wouldn't have been my birthing partner and thus earned himself godfather status.

So it all worked out for the best in the end.

JENNY ON ADAM

He's funny. Quite good looking, though not as much as he likes to think. Oh, and he's not big on cleanliness.

FANTASY FOOTBALL

Pete is hardly at the top of the food chain at work, but sometimes he works late. He came home the other night bouncing with excitement. He even said he'd had lunch with one of the deputy under-managers he reports to.

I had visions of promotions, more money and holidays abroad with the Tiddler.

"What did he say?"

"He said yes. He said yes!" Like the bloody man from Del Monte.

"Yes, what?"

"Yes, I can run a department Fantasy Football league, and he wants to submit a team! I've already chosen mine. It's called Gifford Wanderers and with Cole and Shearer up front, and Phil Neville and..."

I lost interest. Pete's life is a fantasy. Promotion is just a dream and my idea that he loves his work is pure wishful thinking.

We all went on holiday together for the Millennium. It was quite rugged but very beautiful. We had wood fires, which meant the boys had to chop the wood. We girls just lined up to watch our fearless menfolk battle with the great outdoors. I did the John Motson bit.

"OK, let's see what you can do."

"Points for style," said Karen.

"And physique," added Rachel.

"Our first contestant is rugged outdoor type David Marsden. Look at those shoulders, honed to perfection on the golf course."

David swung his axe.

"And it's all over! With one devastating blow! Marsden setting the early pace."

Next was Adam.

"The next contestant, Adam Williams, is playing safe. He's taking on a wood chip. Has he bitten off more than he can chew?"

Adam sliced the wood in half. Devastating dexterity.

"Oh, a masterful performance, silencing the critics." But not us girls, of course.

"And now, the peoples' favourite. They don't call him the Axeman for nothing. Whole forests quake at the sound of his footfall. Prepare for a masterclass in lumberjacking."

We will draw a veil over Pete's performance. I will merely record that the three of us girls had to change our knickers after watching his epic struggle with a twig.

David's great. For a guy with the Financial Times stuffed up his arse. And he knows how to organise a holiday.

KAREN MARSDEN

I'm Karen. I'm an editor. And a mother. And a housewife. And an employer.

I'm editor to Alexander Welch. You know, the Booker
Prize winner? "Blanket of Tears" – the scene where
she's ironing? Rachel said she read it with one hand.

I'm mother to Josh. My own dear little Josh. Bright as a
button. Happy and smiling even when there's no reason
to be. I love him completely. He's the one man I can
rely on completely.

I'm a housewife too. David is many things, but he's
not a househusband.

I'm the employer of Ramona, our nanny. Her English is
improving, but probably not as fast as Josh's Spanish.

Sometimes I wish life wasn't so...

Predictable.

David's predictable. Except when I thought he was
having an affair with Ramona, but he wasn't.

And when he lost his job and decided to be a househusband instead.

And when he remembered our wedding anniversary.

And when he made friends with Adam and Pete
because Rachel is my best friend.

Maybe he's not predictable. Maybe I'm predictable.
Thirty looming up. Married, one son. Life passing me by.

Life's a compromise, I guess.

You can be whoever you want. If you're not happy with who you are, become someone else.

RAMONA

My own personal Spirit of the Beehive is Ramona, our nanny. As Spanish girls go, she is very Spanish. But Josh loves her and she loves Josh.

She is still learning English. Two years on and she has no more than a passing acquaintance with the language, although I suppose Manchester is not the best place to learn the language of Shakespeare. It's the language of David Beckham and Shaun Ryder as well.

Josh can sing "Ten Green Bottles" now, although the version he has learnt is only loosely based on the traditional nursery rhyme. Ramona's version goes:

Ten grin bottool hankin fron de wool
Ten grin bottool hankin fron de wool
An eff one grin bottool shood dud de duh de full
There would only be...
(Long pause while she looks for somebody to help her out. Josh usually comes to her aid)
Nine grin bottool hankin fron de wool!

She gets very upset if anybody encroaches on her territory. In the unlikely event that David takes Josh to the park, she mopes.

"He no here! All day! How I do my job? A nanny with no child?"

Is like a fish without a bicycle, as Rachel so wisely remarked.

Ramona is also a major reason why BT makes profits of £135 a minute.

Cold Fëët

RAMONA'S SEX LIFE

Ramona conducts her sex life over the telephone, which makes it rather more expensive for us than other forms of bodily gratification, like belonging to Manchester's most exclusive health club, or life membership of Royal Lytham & St. Anne's Golf Club. The phone sex mainly concerns a young man called Javier. Javier has been sighted at our house, and apart from the fact that he never washes, he seems to be pleasant enough.

Ramona has certain strange fetishes. However these do not include being sexually harassed by David, which we discovered by unfortunate experience. Just because Ramona was wearing one of my dresses that I had given her, David thought that her bum looked like mine, and molested it. I accepted his excuse, even though he has past form. He once got into bed with me thinking I was Ramona, and whispered sweet nothings in Spanish until he realised it was me in Ramona's bedroom. I'm not sure if Ramona has ever really trusted David since.

"I love the sound of rain," she said once, "thrashing against the window." Impressive and evocative use of the word "thrashing". "It make me wanna run outside with no clothes on."

Adam was obviously taken with this idea. "Really?" he said. "Because the forecast isn't good."

Karen on films

When I was at university – I read History of Art at Birkbeck College, London – we had a one year optional course on "Modern European Film". Most of the films were out of focus and so recent that they were neither historical nor artistic, so it had little bearing on the rest of the course. Maybe that's why I enjoyed it so much.

Have you ever seen "El Espiritu De La Colmena"? It's a Spanish film. In English, it means "The Spirit Of The Beehive". It's a wonderful, touching film about two little girls in a village in Castile in 1940. Well, it's not really about the two little girls, but they drive the action, such as it is. It revolves around the Frankenstein story and an escaped convict and the girls' father, who has a beehive. And their mother who writes letters all day to people who don't exist.

It's beautiful. it's poetic. It's essentially Spanish and entirely universal. It tells us about the human condition.

Karen on music

I'm not sure that music is a big part of our lives. David couldn't tell Elvis from the Wombles and even though he bought the latest CD/DVD/Minidisc equipment, I'm not sure that we've worked out how to use it yet.

I do like Ladysmith Black Mambazo. I got into them through Paul Simon's "Graceland" and also – of course – the television advertisement. But I've got a couple of their CDs which I play in the kitchen when I'm trying to get Josh to eat something. If it works on the advertisement getting the kids to eat, then it ought to work for me.

And have you heard the Soweto String Quartet? "Zebra Crossing?" Now that is real music for the world.

PARENTHOOD

As I said to Jenny
when she first asked
me about life after
becoming a mother,
the word "life" will
no longer apply. You
simply exist to meet
your child's every
demand.

Don't get me
wrong. I wouldn't
have it any other
way. But I'm not
sure if I'd want
another one either.
I know I always said
I wanted three
children, but that
was before I had
one.

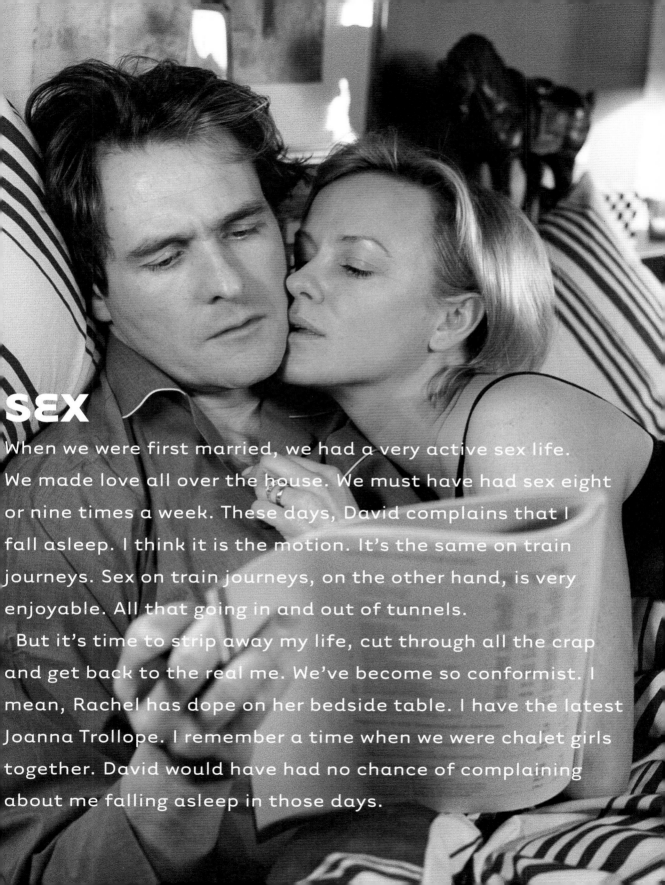

SEX

When we were first married, we had a very active sex life. We made love all over the house. We must have had sex eight or nine times a week. These days, David complains that I fall asleep. I think it is the motion. It's the same on train journeys. Sex on train journeys, on the other hand, is very enjoyable. All that going in and out of tunnels.

But it's time to strip away my life, cut through all the crap and get back to the real me. We've become so conformist. I mean, Rachel has dope on her bedside table. I have the latest Joanna Trollope. I remember a time when we were chalet girls together. David would have had no chance of complaining about me falling asleep in those days.

Hey! Life's a compromise

DAVID'S FAULTS

David does not have many faults. Unless you count desertion, mental cruelty, trying to shag the nanny and being too polite to tell you what he really thinks. It's his public school upbringing. But I had a convent education, and convent girls have no such qualms.

He does not appreciate what it takes to be a working mother.

"Editing takes time", I tell him when he comes home expecting a three-course dinner to be on the table, just waiting for the master of the house to turn up.

"Surely you just press spell-check. How difficult can children's books be? There are less than ten words a page."

I bit my tongue and did not remind him that it should be "fewer than ten words a page", although if one of my authors had made that mistake, the red pen would have come out.

"Precisely. So each one has to be chosen carefully."

LIKE HUSBANDS.

Cold Fèèt

COOKING WITH DAVID AND RAMONA

David is not a naturally domesticated animal. He has no idea whether we have an ironing board, and if so, where it is kept. He cannot tell the pepper from the oregano and he has no knowledge of whether dishwashers have been invented yet.

Ramona cooks Spanish omelette and paella, and occasionally wraps a fish in silver foil and creates something which tastes good, especially when washed down with David's best Montrachet and a couple of packets of Immodium. **David and Josh tried Parmesan Chicken Bake once. I have no idea why.** David bought all the ingredients, except the chicken. By the time he had come back from the supermarket with several chicken pieces to complete the recipe, Josh had got into the flour.

"Place the chicken breasts between clear sheets of film, and flatten with a rolling pin to a thickness of five millimetres." David enjoyed battering the chicken breasts, but then had to go and look for a ruler to measure the thickness. Josh's Mr. Men ruler was covered in peanut butter, but it was still just about usable and it imparted an extra something to the taste of the finished product.

Josh was now covered in bread crumbs and peanut butter, and some marmalade he was dipping his crayons into.

"Take the tomato sauce prepared earlier…"

Before David could register that he had not prepared the tomato sauce earlier, Ramona wandered into the kitchen looking for Josh. I suspect that it is at moments like this that she learns those words I have been trying to persuade her not to repeat in polite company.

David took out his wallet and waved several notes at Ramona. A deal was quickly struck and Ramona took over as head chef.

Ramona likes it when David decides to be a househusband. She earns so much in overtime, bonuses and danger money.

Books I have edited

Before Josh was born, I was a good editor. I edited all sorts of books. When I went back to work I was put onto children's books.

MILLIE THE MOUNTAIN BIKE. Not a completely satisfactory work of literature. Focus groups showed that Stanley the Sports Car was a more popular character than our heroine Millie, and that the moment when he blew his exhaust into her face was the high spot of the book for most of our readers. I do not think that the characterisation is working properly.

ALEXANDER WELCH. His new novel, the follow-up to his Booker Prize winning "Blanket of Tears" is the book I am proudest of. Madeleine and Patrick are two brilliant characters, fully developed, real people. Alec even dedicated the book to me. He's a shit, but he's also a great writer, and he says I give great edit. He gives great word. Just remember it's fiction, not the truth.

LIKE FATHER LIKE SON by Adam Williams (unpublished, and likely to stay that way). Adam's book written "from life". He said he wanted me to be brutal. Although we are friends, he wanted my professional opinion. So I gave it to him.

"What can I say? It left me speechless. It reminds me of what Truman Capote said of Jack Kerouac – 'This isn't writing, it's typing.' In your case, not even good typing. There's a simile in chapter five I quite liked, though of course it's not original. The rest is just wastepaper."

I feel quite proud to have been instrumental in ending Adam's writing career before it had got properly started.

Cold Fëët

TRAINSPOTTING by Adam Williams

(unfinished, unpublished, unreadable)
A good title, maybe, but the bits that
Rachel told me about prove that the
title was the only good word in the
whole book (or half book: he never
finished it).

"Night. Winter. Dark. Cold. The howl
of a dog, an anthem of despair. A
distant sound. Growing louder. Choo
choo choo!"

And more in the same vein. "Pumping
pistons. Rattling rails. Iron horse." It
never got any better.

Alexander Welch and me — our relationship is
based entirely on fiction and dreams (his
fiction my dreams).

KAREN ON DAVID

David's a remarkable man. He's kind and loving, not always good at showing it, but that's what he is. It's not that people dislike him. They just find him a little intense. Playing milk monitor the whole time. He's the same as his father. Emotional openness is not a feature of the Marsden family. Even David's brother Nick took four days to get to the point of his unannounced visit to us, which was, not surprisingly, a loan. David's father is proud of him, and I'm proud of him. I love him.

He was there for Josh's birth, too. Even cancelled a meeting. That's true love.

MONEY

David is not always good with money. Take his African adventure, for example. There was this chap he knew in the city, who asked David if he wanted to invest in a golf course. In Africa. There are very few golf courses in Africa, a fact not unconnected with the fact that there are very few golfers in Africa, but David said there was a rising urban elite, who would play on his course. Unfortunately, this urban elite did not rise enough to get above the floods that inundated the entire area, and they were also rather too elite for the Marxists who staged a coup a few weeks after David's money had been so securely invested. So that was £15,000 gone.

I have no idea whether David has also invested in Saudi off-licences or Teheran night clubs, but I do know he has a few shares in Euro-bloody-Tunnel. This is a man to whom others flock to hear his advice on the stock market. They even pay him for these words of wisdom. I know all consultants are bullshitters, but David must be world class.

Luckily, the Inland Revenue came up with a £1,000 tax rebate at the same time so I took charge of it, even though David made it clear that "fiscal prudence is not your forte", to quote the man to whom I plighted my troth for richer and for poorer. I put it into a building society. One with a blue carpet. It seemed like a pleasant enough place.

And a month later, it turned itself into a bank, doubling our money at a stroke. They had to get rid of the blue carpet as that was no longer the corporate colour, but I never go in there any more so I don't really mind.

That's how to pay for a skiing holiday, not by messing about on golf courses on another continent.

DINNER PARTY CONVERSATION
Suitable subjects for discussion at dinner parties include:

1. Why you must have an Aga, even in a terraced house in Manchester.

2. Which of the Greek islands is in this year? Cephalonia seems to be the front runner, but there's always Kos, Lesbos and Mykonos.

3. Which colour is the new black? Or the old black. It looked like it would be maroon, but it seems that dinner party opinion is moving towards grey. Very dull, grey.

4. Has anybody been to that new restaurant on Deansgate?

5. Children. But only if they have recently achieved something major, like not soiling their nappies for half an hour or learning a new word. Josh learned "bugger" the other day, but I didn't tell anybody about it.

6. Nannies. You take your nanny skiing and the cost really mounts up. If you leave her at home you still have to pay her, and it's when you are on holiday you want your nanny most.

7. Who'd like a little spliff?

8. Did you know, there's a tribe in Borneo where instead of shaking hands on a deal, the men masturbate one another?

Cold Feet

You know what you should do when you're feeling down? Something wild! A tattoo or something. They don't hurt much. No more than childbirth.

A little spliff

When you are already pissed, when you are at a dinner party and you think that you've died and gone to hell — or worse, that you are still here and this is your life — you need Rachel. Her advice is always to roll a joint. She keeps her dope in her bedside table, second drawer down. A home from home.

David was very cross.

"Were you out of your mind?"

"Only briefly. It wasn't very good stuff."

He said afterwards that he had never been so embarrassed. I had to remind him of the school nativity play when one of the three wise men wet himself. His mother told me about it.

SHOPPING LIST

Balsamic vinegar
Feta cheese
Rocket
Bread (white uncut)
Butter (unsalted)
Dijon mustard
Patum Peperium
Plain flour
2 red peppers
Taramasalata
Fresh Dill
Baby food for Josh
That Jil Morgan dress
Hello! magazine
Pregnancy test kit

PETE AND ADAM'S SCHOOL REUNION

Do not ask how I got there, but for reasons not unconnected with moral blackmail, I accompanied Adam to his school reunion a few weeks ago. It was all a bit low rent, like something out of "Carrie".

School reunions are for people who have done well to show off to those who haven't, but it became clear pretty quickly that the entire Class of '86 had not done well. I mean, Pete was one of the high achievers.

So Adam and I changed our lives. He introduced me to everybody as his personal assistant.

"And masseuse," I ad libbed.

"And helicopter pilot." I think Adam has a thing about women in uniform.

"After I left the Foreign Legion," said Adam to some estate agent with a timid wife, "I became a bodyguard to the Sultan of Pashtuk."

"The one who was assassinated." Can't have Adam making everybody believe he's a success.

"It was my day off." He's quick, I'll give him that.

KEEPING SECRETS

Some things are better left unsaid, and some things just have to be revealed. Openness and honesty, that's the thing. David doesn't always agree.

"I can't believe you broke a confidence!" would be his reaction.

"Adam broke it first."

"That doesn't excuse you!"

"I don't need excusing! I'm the only one who's been open and honest. Not that I expect to be thanked. I realise they are not qualities people put much store by nowadays."

I can't stand hypocrisy. We spend time with people we don't like. And tell lies to those we do.

chool reunions are for
eople who have done
ell to show off to
hose who haven't

Holidays

Val d'Isere. -Tuesday
Dear Raich (and Adam)
The snow is great and
the ski instructor has
a great bum. I've pers
uded David to stop
making calls to the office
— threw his mobile down
a mountain, started an
Avelanch. He's much
more relaxed now, and
even took Josh snowbo-
arding. Ramona has
found someone to take
her mind off Javier.
Back on Sunday.
much love
karen, (+ David, Josh,
Ramona)

Mrs Rachael Bradle
17, Shakespear Road
Didsbury
Manchester M17
Angleterre

SALMON Cameracolour Post Card

TEL: [01732] 452381

Printed in England © J. SALMON LTD., SEVENOAKS, KENT.

Clovelly
North Bovey   East Budleigh   Hope Cove
Cockington
Croyde
2 — 47 — 00 — 20   103

5 012493 020

Cold Fëet

NICK

David has never really got on with his brother, Nick. David even calls him Nicholas, which hardly exudes warmth. But it's understandable, I suppose. For eight years he was the apple of his parents' eye, the centre of their world. Then one day he woke up to find the earth had shifted. He'd been pushed to the edge, his position usurped by what he described once as "a mewling, puking cuckoo". Suddenly he had to share his parents' love.

"He's always been spoilt," is what David says about Nick. "Always had whatever he wanted. A new bike, a second-hand car. I had to work for things. I had a paper round when I was eleven."

I told him I couldn't imagine him cycling round delivering papers.

"I didn't. My mother gave me a lift. Well, the roads were dangerous. But that's not the point."

The reason Nick irritates David nowadays is that Nick just drifts through life, and everything comes easily to him. To David, he's inconsiderate and irresponsible and people seem to find it charming. But he doesn't understand that rogues can be lovable.

David's not a rogue: nobody could be less roguish outside a convention of Chief Constables held in a nunnery. But he's lovable.

Rachel's always been what you might call perceptive.

SHOPPING LIST

From the desk of David Marsden:

```
BUY:    10,000 BT at no more than 998p
        25,000 Wilshaw at no more than 48p
all the Mid Kent Water you can get at 600p or less

SELL:   10,000 Smiths Industries at no less than 900p
        50,000 BSkyB — see if you can get 590p


Get out of Wyatt — sell the lot asap.
```

THE MILLENNIUM

You must have plans for the Millennium. I want to spend the Millennium with the people I consider my closest friends. I want it to be something special. Something we'd remember and cherish for the rest of our lives.

Yet for perhaps the most historic moment of our lives, Adam and Rachel said they'd be going to some party they'd rather miss, while Pete and Jenny planned to be at home watching television. We decided to go away. Rent a place. Invite a few people to join us.

At that point Adam said that sounded nice.

"I thought you didn't want to do anything special."

"No, but... well, you should be friends, shouldn't you?"

"Yes. The question is which friends to invite."

I just want people to enjoy themselves. But you can't force them to.

SPORTS AND FITNESS

As a management consultant, I no longer have time for the sports I used to play at Uni (Durham – Politics and Economics, a good 2:2). I've almost completely given up karate, even though I reached black belt level and learnt a few words of Japanese along the way. Nowadays it's squash with Adam, who I can usually beat. If Adam wins the first two games, we play the best of five. If I win the first two, we play best of three.

He's a bit of a wet with his injuries. I've been hit in the balls and it doesn't hurt that much. Used to happen all the time when I was young. A little tap in the gonads, that's all. One of the advantages of a public school education.

I also play golf with Pete from time to time. I can always beat him. He doesn't play often enough to become good at the game, but then he doesn't have the chance to get involved in charity golf days, or rounds with the chairman. I don't think he even knows who his chairman is. And I am absolutely certain that his chairman does not know who Pete is. Just one of the drones, as he is happy to admit. He needs ambition, that chap. Drive.

SCHOOLDAYS

I went to a good school: well, two good schools, the prep school and the public school.

> Dear mummy and daddy,
> Thank you for your last letter. I'm glad everything is well at home. I am doing well this term, and am in the cricket team, which is captained by Curtis minor. I will bat number six and hope to bowl occassionally sometimes. I got 17 out of 20 in the French test with Madame Defarge. Do you know what gender sasifrage is?
> Your loving son,
> David
> P.S Mummy, Daddy come quickly.
> There's buggery in the school.

The P.S. was supposed to provoke some reaction, but all my parents did was increase my allowance. I suppose I was meant to buy the buggers off. I hated that school. Never settled in.

APOLOGIES

I think I am very graceful in the way that I accept apologies. I make it easy for those who have done the wrong thing to put it right. I don't even mind apologising to others if and when I do something wrong.

But I draw the line at apologising on behalf of others, or insisting on an apology when one is not due. As I said to Natalie the moment she raised the subject the day after her dress had been extinguished at that charity do, Jenny doesn't owe you an apology and I'm not going to ask her for one. I'm loyal to my friends. Loyalty may not be something Natalie respects or even recognises, but for me it's something to be valued.

CHARITY

I spend a lot of money on charity. For instance, Karen's dress for the big function with Natalie and Bill (her third husband, the one before George) was a Prada and had a price tag with more noughts on the end than is good for a man's bank balance, but it was worth every penny. And anyway we wrote it off against tax.

Then there was my new evening suit, new shoes and new shirt and bow tie so we won't have any change out of a thousand pounds for that lot. You must admit, that's a big contribution to charity for just one evening.

Charity and work tend to mix, of course. Evenings like that are not social occasions, even though we take our spouses. Strictly business, for charitable causes.

Karen gave that dress to Ramona a year or so later, as she said she'd never wear it again, and might as well give it to a good cause. I told her if she wanted to help a good cause, why not give it to the starving in Africa? They're already as thin as supermodels, and now they can dress like them.

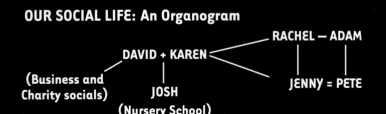

OUR SOCIAL LIFE: An Organogram

RACHEL — ADAM

DAVID + KAREN

(Business and Charity socials)

JOSH
(Nursery School)

JENNY = PETE

Don't bring me problems, solve them.

KEEPING SECRETS

Life is about keeping secrets. Open relationships don't work. I don't want to know everything that goes on in Karen's life, and I certainly don't want her to find out everything that goes on in mine. That would just be dull, and whatever life may throw at us, I hope that dullness isn't the one thing that sticks.

But there's a time and place for secrets. Suppose you knew the husband of a friend of yours was having an affair. Should you tell your friend? Karen says you wouldn't be much of a friend if you didn't.

On the other hand, if, for instance, you were impotent – temporarily – would you tell the whole world? No, of course you wouldn't. Although, like a fool, I did the next best thing. I told Adam.

MOBILE PHONES

I don't know how we managed before the invention of mobile phones. How can a man run his life without being able to contact the right people at the right time?

At the airport, for example, all I have to do is to ring home and I can tell Karen the reason for the delay wherever I may be in the world. It's usually Frankfurt. Dreadful airport. No decent children's toys in the duty-free section. Not that duty-free means anything these days in Europe.

It does in Japan, where I've had to go a couple of times recently, but the mobile doesn't seem to work there. Probably fortunate, as the cost would be horrendous, I expect. But speaking to Japan from England – for example outside the church when Pete and Jenny's Adam was being christened – is only possible when you have a mobile phone. You see the Japanese work in a different time zone, so they work when we don't and vice versa. They also work in a different language, and if there isn't a Japanese person just passing by at the time to help with the translation, then it can get difficult. What does "Bakayaro" mean, anyway?

One final rule on mobile phones: Don't lend them to Ramona. That's a quicker way to use up your life savings than investing in Central African golf courses, as Karen will persist in reminding me.

THE WORK/HOME LIFE BALANCE

It's easy to get the right balance between our working lives and our home lives. For instance, Josh's bedtime story is often a company report. It's not the story he needs, it's the soothing sound of his father's voice as he drifts into the security of a dreamless sleep.

"And in the third quarter, the gross profit margin rose to 24%! Isn't that a lot! On an annual turnover of just seven and a half million pounds! What's more, the sale of the warehousing division netted £136,000, leading to overall debt — oh dear, whoops-a-daisy — on the current account of £250,000." The only trouble with that system is that it sends me to sleep more quickly than it does Josh.

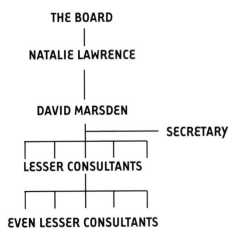

THE OFFICE: An Organogram

THE BOARD

NATALIE LAWRENCE

DAVID MARSDEN ———— SECRETARY

LESSER CONSULTANTS

EVEN LESSER CONSULTANTS

RAMONA

I'm not quite sure how we came to employ Ramona. I know that
Karen came crashing into the office when I was conducting a seminar on hardball negotiating skills, and demanded that we hire a
nanny. I'm not quite sure how she came to get her way: after all, I
was the one running the seminar, not her, but we ended up with a
Spanish girl with a highly developed sex drive and a telephone
glued to her ear.

  "Scusita", she says all the time.
  And then there's "I theenk I tek my keetchen in the lunge, OK?"
  Or "Forgive to interrupt, but..." No wonder Josh is inarticulate.
  Karen is thrilled when Ramona manages to use the past tense. I
have no idea how she can tell whether any particular word from the
selection of strange sounds that tumble from Ramona's mouth is
in the past tense or the dative case or the pluperfect subjunctive.
But Karen is an editor, so she can tell.
  But all in all, Ramona is a Good Thing. Her efforts are easily
overlooked but shouldn't be undervalued.

SƐX

If there's one thing I should have learnt from being married to Karen, and from watching how people like Adam and Jenny get things all wrong, it's that you shouldn't write anything down that you don't want others to know. So I hope Karen is not reading this.

I did briefly suffer from a bout of impotence. I read a book about it – "Keeping Up" by Oskar Zengler, which started promisingly but doesn't live up to expectations. Asking Adam for advice was a very stupid move, so in the end I sought professional help. I went to see Trixie, a prostitute with a card in a phone booth and a flat above a door in a dingy alleyway. She wasn't cheap but she was worth every penny.

We didn't do anything. I love Karen. More than that. I'm in love with Karen. She makes me look great when I dance, and not many people can do that. I think she's gorgeous.

Trixie just told me that we are all the same, stressed out in high powered jobs. She's had them all, a judge, a surgeon, a management consultant – make that two management consultants including me. Get on top of your job and you'll be on top of your sex life as well, she said. Her judge pulled himself together, sent down a few criminals for good long stretches and was soon back in the arms of his secretary, fully functional again.

That's what I did too. Just took control of my life again. I know Karen appreciated it.

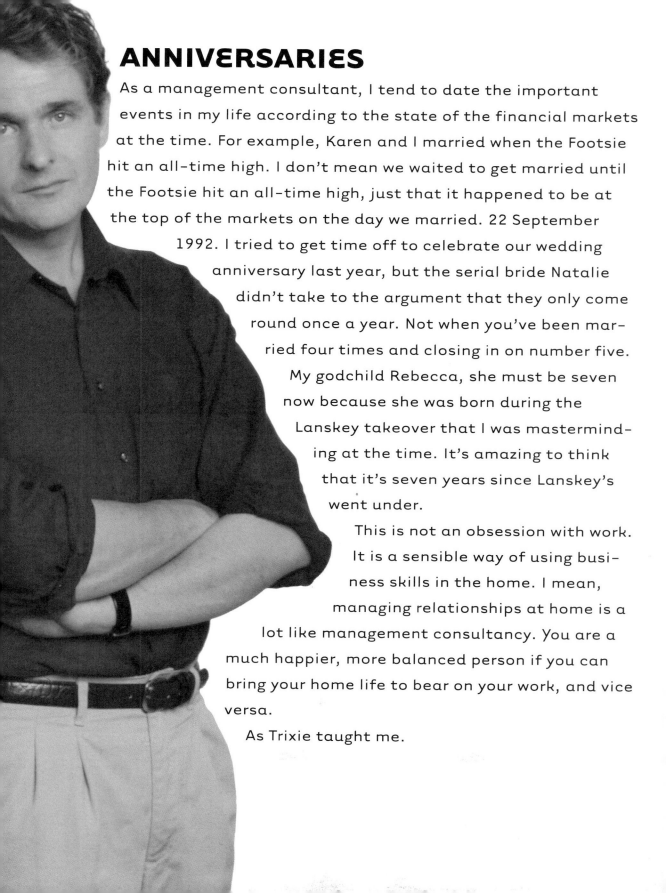

ANNIVERSARIES

As a management consultant, I tend to date the important events in my life according to the state of the financial markets at the time. For example, Karen and I married when the Footsie hit an all-time high. I don't mean we waited to get married until the Footsie hit an all-time high, just that it happened to be at the top of the markets on the day we married. 22 September 1992. I tried to get time off to celebrate our wedding anniversary last year, but the serial bride Natalie didn't take to the argument that they only come round once a year. Not when you've been married four times and closing in on number five. My godchild Rebecca, she must be seven now because she was born during the Lanskey takeover that I was masterminding at the time. It's amazing to think that it's seven years since Lanskey's went under.

This is not an obsession with work. It is a sensible way of using business skills in the home. I mean, managing relationships at home is a lot like management consultancy. You are a much happier, more balanced person if you can bring your home life to bear on your work, and vice versa.

As Trixie taught me.

DAVID ON FILMS

I don't know much about films. Karen and I have different tastes, so we don't go to the cinema much together. And I don't like going on my own.

My favourite of all time is "Bridge On The River Kwai". Alec Guinness and Jack Hawkins and William Holden. And Sessue Hayakawa as the Japanese camp commandant. I don't think the Japanese are much like that these days. We do a lot of business with the Japanese.

It was filmed in Ceylon, Sri Lanka as it is now. I like it because Alec Guinness stands for all the values that my father believes in - that I believe in too - like getting on with the job without complaining, like finishing the task and tolerating impossible situations in a stoical way. Dealing with foreigners too. The American was as bad as the Japanese.

It's like with Ramona. She's not easy, but we do it without complaining.

DAVID ON MUSIC

I don't really understand modern music. Gorecki I can relate to, and Rodrigo's Guitar Concerto de Aranjuez, but I'm not too sure about rock music – you know, R.E.M., Boyzone and 2Pac Somebody. I'm a Shostakovitch man. Or Moussorgsky.

I wanted to take Karen to a show in London for our wedding anniversary, so I asked Rachel for advice.

"There's the question of which show to see. I wondered about 'Cats'."

"So do most people who've seen it," said Rachel, unhelpfully.

"'Phantom Of The Opera'?"

Rachel pulled a face in the way that only Rachel can.

"'Starlight Express'?"

No response.

"'Whistle Down The Wind'?"

"David, how many Andrew Lloyd Webber musicals has Karen seen?"

"None, I think."

"Spot on!", said Rachel, her finger pointing ominously at my heart.

"Not Andrew Lloyd Webber." I can take a hint.
In the end I got tickets for Judi Dench's new play. It wasn't a musical.

Cold Feet

DAVID: PRIORITIES

1. Karen (obviously)

2. Josh (or first equal. Obviously)

3. Work. Management consultancy (except when it gets in the way of my friends)

4. My friends (except when they get in the way of my work)

5. Wine. I have a good cellar. It's not what I'd call a fine cellar yet, but it will be.

6. Sport. Squash and golf especially. I can't stand football.

7. My parents. I forgot them. Perhaps they should go a bit higher on the list.

8. My brother Nick. I didn't forget him.

I don't want to give the impression that reading the newspaper is a higher priority than talking to my brother Nick, but it is when a) the newspaper has the latest news of the impending MBO at CDTL and the reshuffle at Thomas Alexander, and b) my brother Nick is summoning up the courage to ask me for a loan.

FATHERHOOD

I wouldn't call it demanding, this fatherhood thing. In fact, I hardly noticed a change in the first couple of years after Josh was born. I think these things tend to get a bit exaggerated.

But there comes a time when every man needs to learn a few tricks of the Dad trade. I offer the following advice:

1. BAA BAA BLACK SHEEP - full lyrics, authorised version

Baa Baa Black Sheep, have you any wool?
Yes sir, yes sir, three bags full.
One for the master, one for the dame
And one for the little boy that lives down the lane!
(The rhyming is a bit feeble: I mean, "dame" and "lane". No wonder it takes a bit of time to learn all the words.)

2. THE POWER OF McDONALDS

Two of Josh's first words were "chocolate" and "milkshake", occasioned by my offer to take him to McDonald's for lunch. He will soon be able to say "cheeseburger", a three-syllable word which I am sure young Timothy Boyd has not yet mastered. And they provide plenty of paper towels to mop up after small children have been sick.

3. DONKEY RIDES ON BLACKPOOL BEACH

Children seem to like this. Well, Josh does anyway. Especially when it is followed up by a portion of chips from the motorway services on the way home.

Cold Feet

JOSH

How is Josh doing compared with other kids? Pretty well, I'd say.

Talking:

Reasonably advanced. Still uses baby words like "choo-choo" but came up with a wonderful sentence in the bank the other day: "I've got a knicker problem." Not many children of his age could have managed that.

Walking and muscle co-ordination:

Runs all over the place these days, and can throw his food quite a distance. Has a good left hook, as young Timothy Boyd found out the other day. "Poor little Timothy" as the principal of the nursery school calls him, is minding his own business, colouring or whatever, when Josh wanders up and wallop! But Timothy Boyd is older than Josh, and bigger. Well done Josh, I say.

Social skills:

Regrettable tendency to soil his pants and the carpet, not to mention almost any other object within range, but at least he seems to enjoy doing it. According to the head of his nursery school (and what does she know about it? I doubt if she's ever had children, or even been in a position which might have rendered the subsequent bearing of children likely), antisocial tendencies are not uncommon when children lack siblings to keep them in check. But Karen and I are working on that.

MARRIAGE

I remember an argument my parents had when I was young. It was probably nothing but to me and my brother it was the end of the world. I mean, summer holidays are meant to be happy, aren't they? We had visions of them splitting up, each taking one of us. Of course, by supper it was all forgotten.

I don't think people should stay together for the sake of their kids. They should stay together for the sake of each other. I mean, every marriage goes through its bad patches, but that's all they are - patches. Well, not always, but you got to give yourself time to find out.

Women have been housewives for centuries. Now it's my turn.

Cold Fëët

Age doesn't matter, except with whisky.

Hello. David Marsden. Management consultancy, that's me.

Karen says I'm a bullshitter, but that's what I'm paid to be. Natalie Lawrence - that's who I work for... er... with — pays me very well for being a bullshitter.

And I'm a black belt at karate. I don't get paid for that.

That's how I met Karen. She's my wife. It was at a party. Some prat was bothering her, so I kind of rescued her. A knight in shining armour, she thought I was. It's nice when somebody thinks you're great.

We were married on 22 September 1992. Or was it 93? No, it was 1992. The day the Footsie 100 hit an all-time high. Easy to remember really. It was the happiest day of my life.

MY HOME LIFE: An Organogram

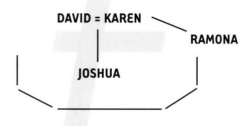

I love Karen. And I love Josh, my son. Our son.

We also have Ramona, the nanny. She is quite good with Josh, but not very good with the English language. This causes misunderstandings sometimes, but that's all they are. Misunderstandings.

I also have a brother, Nicholas. He's much younger than me, what many people would call an accident but I'd say he was a mistake. He's always been my parents' favourite, getting away with things that I wouldn't even dream of attempting. He has no sense of responsibility, no sense of purpose. A man's got to have a sense of purpose.

Karen's best friend is Rachel, and although I like Rachel very

much, she brings in her wake people like Adam, Pete and Jenny. Don't get me wrong, I like them all very much, but I'm not sure how much I want everybody to know that I like them. Or even that I know them. They are hardly the most refined of our friends.

Natalie doesn't like Pete and Jenny very much, but that could be linked to the time that Jenny let off a fire extinguisher all over her at a ball we were all attending. She says she thought the wife was stupid, but the husband must be missing a chromosome. That's a bit harsh maybe, but I can see her point sometimes.

Cold Fëët

David Marsden

TRIVIA QUESTIONS AND ANSWERS

The Nag's Head Trivia Machine is about as near as I get to sport these days, apart from traipsing around the golf course behind David. Gets the competitive juices flowing, at least.

   Along with the beers.

1. Which was the first British city to have pavements?
   - a) Leeds
   - b) Edinburgh
   - c) Bristol

2. What were Blur originally called?
   - a) Seymour
   - b) The Unfocussed
   - c) Aardvarks

3. How many parts did Alec Guinness play in "Kind Hearts And Coronets"?
   - a) 6
   - b) 7
   - c) 8

4. Whose last words were "I shall hear in Heaven"
   - a) Vincent van Gogh
   - b) Ludwig van Beethoven
   - c) Mine, if I don't shut up with these daft quizzes.

had a row with this woman because I parked in space reserved for families. I mean, just ecause I don't have my family with me doesn't mean I'm not shopping for them.

e answers were b), a), c) and b). Jenny's alternative answer c) for number 4 was disallowed

WATCHING TV

Watching television is a major part of anybody's life. It always annoys me how in soaps like East Enders or Coronation Street, they never talk about the telly. I mean, have you ever been into a pub where people are NOT talking about what was on the telly last night, or what's going to be on tonight, and whether it's any good? Only in the bloody Rover's Return and the Queen Vic. They don't even notice the World Cup Final in those pubs. That's what makes soaps unreal for me.

We've got cable now, so I don't have to watch just the terrestrials. I watch everything. I even like the cartoons the Tiddler watches. If ever I'm away from home - management training for example - I like to watch his favourite cartoons because it makes me feel closer to him.

Or we can get in a video. Watched "Enter The Dragon" with Adam the other night. He described it as Men Behaving Sadly.

JENNY WHEN SHE GETS GOING

Marriage to Jenny is not always plain sailing. She has a temper on her, that girl. And a pretty fine right hook. It's not that I often do things wrong, it's just that she would have done things differently.

"I'm going to rip your throat out!" is not the way a man likes to be greeted after a hard day at the office, but marriage is all about for better, for worse, so you keep working at it. And I do love her. Really.

PETE ON JENNY

The thing about Jenny is she's never satisfied. Which I don't mean in a negative way. It's just that she's always striving to make things better. And I allow her to do that. I mean, it's like her waiting to do up the lounge. It doesn't need it. But need isn't the issue. Change is the issue. Stagnate and die. Redecorate and thrive.

I'd do anything for Jenny. Quit my job, let her control the TV remote, give up drinking...

I'd do almost anything for Jenny.

Cold Fëët

THE MILLENNIUM

New Year is worse than Christmas. The Millennium is a thousand times worse than your normal New Year. Who wants to be happy just because of a meaningless moment in time, when you can be as grumpy as you like in the privacy of your own home?

We thought we might have a quiet night in.

In the end, so glad that David had other plans.

Tobacco and other leaves

I used to smoke. To keep my weight down. Jenny said it didn't work and I was only killing myself in small doses, so when the Tiddler was on the way, I gave up.

Jenny never did smoke. Except the occasional joint, with Karen and Rachel. But that's only very occasional, because David doesn't approve. I'm sure he must have tried pot in his younger days (if he had any younger days), but he wouldn't have inhaled. He's quite happy to smoke the occasional cigar, which is much worse for him than a toke or two. All part of the consultant's image, I suppose.

Cold Fëët

THE OFFICE: An Organogram
Audit Department

MANAGER

DEPUTY MANAGER

SECTION CHIEFS

DEPUTY SECTION CHIEFS

ME   OTHER DRONES   AMY

MANAGEMENT DEVELOPMENT

I do not rank very high in the management structure of my firm, and I do not want to. Every time I hear about a training programme "to identify and encourage management potential" or some such bollocks, I run the other way as fast as I can. Unfortunately, that is not always fast enough, even though I represented my school in the Under-12s 100 metres hurdles.

My argument is always that I don't want to be a manager, so why do I have to do it? The answer seems to be, as punishment. With the extra comment that "it's only a weekend". Only a weekend! Don't they realise how precious my weekends with Jenny and baby Adam are? Why couldn't they make it a full week? It must take at least that long to mould the management of tomorrow.

All I do is work on audits. Auditing is a way to make work for yourself without really trying. You find one error and it leads you to a hundred more. It would make for a lot of late nights if I found them all.

FANTASIES

Do you fancy women who work in pubs? The new barmaid at The Nag's Head is sex. She is a pure distillation of man's basic sexual urges. She is fantasy made flesh. When I was younger I had dreams. One of them I remember involved Samantha Fox at a jumble sale.

I inherit it from my Dad. He was a florist, and also a war hero, bootlegger and bull-shitter. He claimed once to have given Frank Sinatra a leg up over a wall in Chorlton-cum-Hardy, when he was doing a concert at the Palace in Manchester. Frank Sinatra, not my Dad. Doing the concert, I mean. I forget why he needed the leg up, and who was chasing them, but I do know that Ol' Blue Eyes was not very grateful. He never even gave my Dad a couple of tickets for the concert.

endship has its ups and downs. Friendship also has its right hooks, which are usually thoroughly deserved. Friends tell one
other everything. Give each other support. The little shit!

Sex

That's another thing about fatherhood. There's always a matching somebody who finds herself involved in motherhood. In my case, Jenny.

Do you fancy women who are mothers? It's difficult to begin with. Elvis went off Priscilla once little Lisa Marie was born, so Priscilla took up with her karate coach. I wouldn't say I've gone off Jenny — because I haven't, and anyway she doesn't have a karate coach. David is a karate black belt, but he doesn't give lessons. But sex is different now.

For a start it's not as frequent. Do you know that stitches take six weeks to heal after childbirth? Ryan Giggs got a really nasty gash on his shin and he was fit to play the following weekend, but Jenny was off games for six weeks.

PETE ON DAVID

David's a bit of a control freak, with his golf lessons and his Cluedo tournaments and all, but he's also very generous and very unselfish. I suppose if I were to meet him for the first time now, I'd think he was a bit of a prat and he'd think I was one. Whereas in fact, we both recognise that Adam actually is a prat.

ITINERARIES

Planning itineraries is something I am very good at. You have to be good at things like that if you want to stay one step ahead of the traffic jams.

The route from home to the hospital when the baby was due was planned in every detail. I worked out that between 8 and 9 in the morning, Tavistock Street is absolutely chocker and you can easily lose twenty minutes. So, you go left into Bradley Street and approach it from the north. In the evening, it's Cross Street that's the problem. It would have worked if it had not been for a few small details:

1. I was playing golf with David at the time, so we didn't start from home.
2. I didn't have my car with me at the golf course.
3. Adam had my mobile, so Jenny couldn't get through to tell me the race was on.
4. There was a burst water main in square H3 of page 57.

Dad could never get it right. He never used the motorways and used to potter along the A34 and then get stuck around Chorlton-cum-Hardy every time. I mean, what can you do with someone who won't embrace the M6? You can easily avoid the roadworks at Knutsford by coming off at Sandbach. Even if you get caught up around Holmes Chapel, it's better than Wilmslow. He used to say two hours door to door isn't bad, but I could knock half an hour off that every time.

GOLF

To be honest, I hate golf. But it's the only social life I'm allowed at the moment. I don't play squash because I can never even take a point off Adam or David, and not even the Sharman's Cross Old Boys Fourth XI football wants me any more. My 100 metres hurdles for the school no longer counts for anything. And you need to keep fit. Walking down to the pub to meet Adam for a swift half does not really count.

I'm not very good at golf, despite David's coaching. I'm the only person I know who needs to borrow a calculator before submitting my scorecard at the end of a round. I'm not yet within striking distance of getting a handicap. My main problem is that I am always within striking distance of the ball, even after I've played my shot.

FOOTBALL

I was the Under-12s goalie. Could have been another Peter Schmeichel, but I never felt I got the support I needed from my captain. Setbacks at that early stage can have a bad effect on anybody's sporting career.

Sharman's Cross School, Wythenshawe
Tel: 061 4379206

UNDER 12s v. St. GREGORY'S MAINE ROAD
12 MARCH 1979. HOME. KICK-OFF 2.30
~~GEORGE WRIGHT~~ ~~CHARLES MOLLEY~~ PETE GIFFORD (GOAL)

ANDREW ROSSDALE
GRAHAM FLOOD
ANTHONY DEAL
DAVID GLENN
CARL READING
JULIAN AYRES
NIGEL COBB
ADAM WILLIAMS (CAPTAIN)
ROBIN QUANTRILL
JAMES FRANKS
RESULT:

LOST 17-3 !!

But not all the goals were my fault. "Pubic" Ayres scored one with a back pass into the top left-hand corner of the net which would have tested Gordon Banks at his peak.

Cold Fëët

CHARITY

Charity means being invited to flash evening functions, and then having to pay for it. It means fishing out your old tuxedo from the back of the wardrobe, and then wondering why the arms have shrunk since you last wore it. It also means wondering why wide lapels fluted with velvet brocade have gone out of fashion. And it means having Jenny comment that she didn't know that wide lapels fluted with velvet brocade were ever in fashion. And it means having to pay for a decent glass of beer because there's nothing free except champagne.

It also means sticking your loose change in the RNLI collecting box in the Nag's Head, and avoiding the collectors who gather outside the supermarket on a Saturday morning like blue-rinsed hyenas closing in on a dead antelope. You can do that by saving last year's poppies or stickers or whatever if you like, to make it look as though you've already been had, but that's more trouble than putting 20p in the pot and applying a new sticker to your shirt.

PARTY TRICKS

Have you ever seen that trick where you set fire to a bit of biscuit paper and then it floats right up to the ceiling? David asked me to show him how to do it once. Jenny and his boss Natalie were arguing quite forcefully about Wyatt's Jammy Mouthfuls at the time, which might have had something to do with David's request.

It doesn't always work. You have to be careful when you light the paper that you don't also set fire to the tablecloth, which is particularly probable if the tablecloth is made of paper, like it was at this cheap but expensive charity function. And also be careful you don't set fire to the table.

Adam's always been a wuss! I remember the time he thought he'd broken his wrist. It was just puberty.

PETE ON ADAM

Adam is not very good with women. Relationship is too long a word for the way he treats them. It's four syllables. The affair would be over before you could finish saying it. But then most women would be over him in minutes, too.

When we were at school, Adam got suspended for putting potassium permanganate in the swimming pool. It was me that grassed on him. I was pissed off because he wouldn't give me Joe Jordan. He was all I needed to finish the set. I never did get Joe Jordan, although I had five swaps of Tony Currie.

SUPERMARKET:
AISLE 1 (Left hand side)

CARROTS (2kg)
CAULIFLOWER (1)
KING EDWARD POTS (5 kg)
TOMATOES (1 pack)

(Right hand side)
  BUNCH OF BANANAS
  4 GRANNY SMITH APPLES
  PLUMS IF RIPE

AISLE 2 (Left hand side)
  TOOTHPASTE
  DEODERANT (M & F)
  RAZOR BLADES
  BABY WIPES
  DISPOSABLE NAPPIES

AISLE 8 (LEFT HAND SIDE)
  BEER (6-pack)
  LAGER (6-pack)
  WHISKY (Adam owes us)
  CRISPS

Cold Fëët

MARRIAGE

Adam says that it's wrong to assume that only married
people can have lasting relationships. Just because people
are married doesn't mean they are happy. Well, he might be
right in some cases, but me and Jenny, we've just had a baby.
He can't tell me that he's never thought about marrying
Rachel. Sometimes it's the only thing he thinks about.
Adam's problem is fear. Of failure.

FILMS

It's difficult to pick a favourite film. I quite like "Klute", you know the film with Jane Fonda and Donald Sutherland, where they're in bed and she's... well, when I was much younger I fancied Jane Fonda.

The first film I ever saw was "The Spy Who Loved Me", and I suppose that's why I've always thought Roger Moore was the best James Bond. "Nobody Does It Better" has always been the best Bond song, and Jaws is the best Bond villain. That's not to say I don't appreciate Sean Connery or Timothy Dalton or Pierce Brosnan or George Lazenby

– in fact there are times when I think his "On Her Majesty's Secret Service" was the best of all.

Diana Rigg was certainly the sexiest Bond girl. Lady. Woman.

No, I can't pick a favourite from the whole Bond ~~ouvre oeuver ouerve~~ genre.

MUSIC

MY FAVOURITE MUSIC? Easy! **Tears For Fears.** "Everybody Wants To Rule the World", "Mad World", "Shout", "Sowing The Seeds Of Love". That was the soundtrack of my adolescence. I play their "Greatest Hits" tape all the time in the car.

And I like Meatloaf too. Ever since "Bat Out Of Hell". I suppose "I'd Do Anything For Love" is his best track, but they all get me right here.

And play it **LOUD.**

FATHERHOOD

It's hell. After a few weeks, I was a complete physical and psychological wreck. It was OK at first, although Jenny wouldn't let me video little Adam's arrival into the world, but from then on it was downhill.

I hate my life. I love the baby, but it's everything that goes with him. Don't babies ever sleep?

It's expensive, too. Do you know that by the age of 18, a child will have cost you a quarter of a million pounds? And, as David remarked, I don't suppose that includes private schools. Or bail. Somehow, I knew Adam would think of that.

PREGNANCY

Several facts you probably did not know about pregnancy. But you ought to. Responsible fatherhood is all about sharing every experience.

1. By the eighth month, the baby is eighteen inches long and weighs five and a half pounds.

2. The placenta is full of vitamins and minerals.

3. The cervix stretches to ten centimetres (four inches) when the top of the baby's head becomes visible. That's called "crowning".

4. When the head crowns, you shouldn't push because if the baby's born too quickly, the mother's skin might tear.

5. When the head appears, the midwife must always check the umbilical cord, to ensure it isn't looped around the baby's neck.

6. Pack the following items in the overnight bag for the hospital: Nightie (XL size); maternity bras (2); dressing gown (warm); slippers (soft but supportive); knickers (at least 4 prs); breast pads; sanitary towels; toothbrush; toothpaste; towels (2); baby clothes (lots, but don't forget you'll be given lots of Babygros by wellwishers long before you leave the hospital); nappies; make-up and hand cream; Chanel no. 5 or similar; a good book (War And Peace – you'll never get another chance to read it).

7. Pregnancy is nature's way of making sure men don't want sex.

I hated school. Sharman's Cross in Wythenshawe. That's where I met Adam. We were always bickering then and we still do now. When I was a kid I used to be able to shut him up by sitting on him. Not so easy now. They don't like you sitting on people in the pub or on a tram.

Jenny and I had our first real snog when I was at Sharman's Cross. Behind the bike sheds, of course. Jenny went to the girls' grammar across the park, because she was pretty bright, and we used to meet after school for a smoke. I've given up smoking now, since the Tiddler came along, but I still snog Jenny. That's more addictive than smoking.

After Sharman's Cross, I went to university. Keele, the only place of learning better known for its motorway service station. I read History, which as I suspected at the time has been of no practical use whatsoever in later life. I did a thesis on "Historical Artifacts" with special reference to Napoleon's penis, which was sold at auction a few years back for some derisory sum.

Now I work for the insurance company, in the audit department. I'm at the bottom of the food chain, with all the other drones. It suits me. Just so long as I never get into management.

I'm Pete. Full name Peter Algernon Gifford.

My father was Algernon too, and so is my son — Adam Preston Algernon Gifford. I know that gives him four initials, but I hope people won't think he's upper class. He's named after my best friend, Adam, who got to the hospital before I did. And Preston, the motorcycle cop, who got to the hospital at the same time that I did — a split second earlier, if anything, as I was riding pillion.

And Algernon, after my Dad. Algernon's been in the family for generations. My great great grandfather was an Algernon, and every Gifford since.

It's not my favourite name. *To be honest, it's ugly, old fashioned and in its shortened form it means "pond scum",* which was one of my nicknames at school. Another was "Smegma".

Three generations of Algernons.

Pete Gifford

There's nothing worse than lying alone in bed listening to someone else in the midst of a multiple orgasm.

I've always had a thing for women who drink straight from the bottle.

DRUGS

Not a good thing. Especially when Rachel smokes a joint when I'm somewhere else, and then accuses me of being middle-aged and hits me when I tell her to grow up. But on the other hand, there's nothing wrong in letting our hair down, while we still have some.

Getting hold of drugs is not always easy. It's a well-known fact that a bouncer (night-club bouncers, not that bloody dog in "Neighbours") is a likely source of supply, but they don't always come across. And Pete doesn't help.

We go to this club, right, and I go, "No-one's drinking alcohol. You know what that means?" and he goes, "Well, er, yeah, they're all driving." I mean, what is he on? Absolutely nothing, that's the trouble.

All we scored was a couple of Tic-Tacs anyway. Twenty quid for a couple of Tic-Tacs. I thought it was odd that they were sugar-coated. Pete thought that was so they'd appeal to children, which when you come to think of it, Tic-Tacs do.

Cold Fëët

Good line that – non-specific, rather like the urethritis that I caught from some less successful liaison a year or two back.

"All that sex and you don't think that we're compatible?" Tears before bedtime, I could tell.

"No. I mean, I like sex as much as the next man. Probably more. But not as much as you. Or not as often, anyway." She was insatiable, that Amy.

"I was just trying to please you. I thought it's what you wanted. It's what men say they want."

"Don't get me wrong, you're great at it. It's probably the practice. But I want more from a relationship." Like the opportunity to have sexual fantasies which are not immediately overtaken by events.

You have to be firm with women like Amy. A man owes it to himself not to be entirely shagged out by the time he is forty.

OFF

The sad truth is that once you're in your thirties, it's well nigh impossible to meet a woman who's both attractive and on her own.

BREAKING IT

It is not easy to say goodbye to somebody. Even though I have had plenty of practice at getting rid of women who still want me long after I've lost interest in them, there's still an art in saying goodbye gracefully.

Remember Amy? As if I could forget her!

"I don't think we should see each other again," was my opening gambit. That usually sets the scene. "I just don't think we are compatible."

Cold Fëët

OUR WONDERFUL POLICE

The Manchester police are wonderful. I have come into contact with them from time to time, and they have always been most fair.

There was the time when young Adam was born. Pete got a lift to the hospital on the back of a police motorcycle. That's how young Adam got the Preston in his name — after Preston the policeman. I wonder if Preston was called that because he was conceived there? Like Brooklyn Beckham, although rather less exotic. Quite possibly.

But then as young Adam Preston Algernon Gifford was not conceived in Preston (as far as I know), the name rather loses its geographical connection in his case.

Then I came across Preston again (thank God it was him and not one of his less enlightened colleagues) when they claimed I was causing a disturbance by wandering around outside Rachel's flat wearing nothing but a rose up my bum. It wasn't a disturbance. It was love in action. I'm glad Preston saw it that way too.

It was love in action again when we met Preston for the third time. That was the night when a joyrider drove through the Oxfam shop window. The only problem was that Rachel and I were in the shop window at the time, in a large double bed. Acting out Rachel's fantasies. Preston was very good about it all, although you might have expected his patience to be wearing just a little bit thin when he saw it was us again.

Then there was the drug dealing charges. Well, Pete's drug dealing charges. I was just brought in as an accessory. Pete doesn't know the first thing about drugs — "So smack is heroin?", he asked me — and it was only his complete ignorance that got us into the fight in the first place. As for the one hundred and forty Ecstasy tablets found in his possession, well only Pete could get away with a defence based on complete naiveté, but the police know a complete dickhead when they see one.

All in all, the Manchester police are a wonderful bunch.

SEX IS FUN. As Woody Allen said, sex is a wonderful thing between two adults who really care for each other. Between three or more, it's fantastic.

It's different for men and women, too. Women just sometimes don't have an orgasm. Or so I've heard it said.

I bought a book once on sexual technique. Advanced sexual technique. It was on the second shelf, behind necrophilia. It was called "Fantastic Sex".

It had an interesting section about acting out your fantasies. We haven't got a hammock, nor a horse, so several of their suggestions were difficult to act out, but Rachel had another idea.

Making love in a shop window.

Inevitably, parents love their children more than their children love them. A father looks at his son and sees a part of himself. They say, "Be careful what you wish for". My wish for my son was that he grow up independent of mind and strong of will. That he has, drives me mad. It also fills me with pride. I know that Pete will be a good father. I've seen the way he looks at his son. With love. A love that only a father can recognise. And which I recognise because it's how I look at Pete.

ADAM'S CHRISTENING SPEECH

"I asked Pete's Dad what it had been like for him to become a father. He sent me this."

Cold Feet

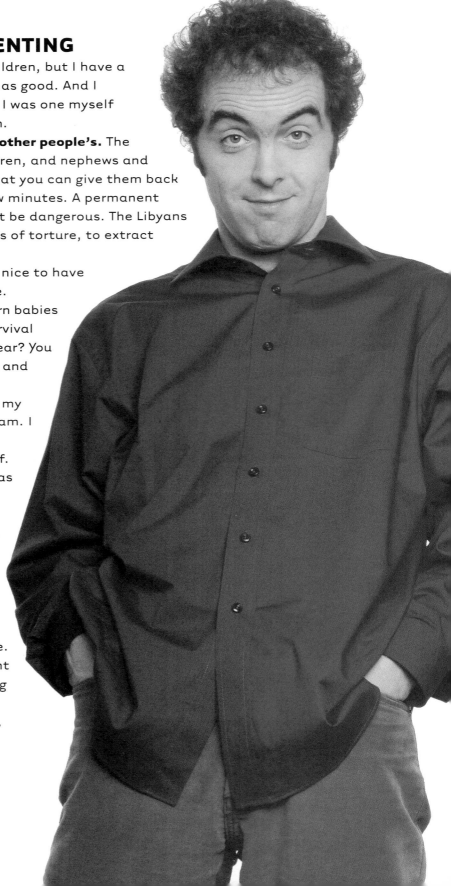

PRACTICAL PARENTING

Yes, I know I don't have children, but I have a godson, and that's almost as good. And I know about kids. After all, I was one myself once. Rachel says I still am.

I love children. **Well, other people's.** The great thing about godchildren, and nephews and nieces too, I suppose, is that you can give them back to their parents after a few minutes. A permanent relationship with one might be dangerous. The Libyans use children as instruments of torture, to extract confessions.

All the same, it would be nice to have one to keep once in a while.

Did you know that newborn babies have a highly developed survival instinct? And no sense of fear? You can get them to grip a rope and they'll know not to let go.

I worry sometimes about my godson and namesake, Adam. I tried hanging him from a washing line, but he fell off. Landed on the washing I was hanging out. Loved it. Giggled happily.

Must be something to do with his genetic make-up. Pete can't hang on to a phone call, let alone a washing line. So I need to be there to teach him all the important things in life. Things even more important than hanging on to washing lines.

I'll be there for him.

GEORGE BEST

Rachel says I think I'm George Best. Well, there are similarities. I haven't got the scruffy beard and the paunch, but definite similarities all the same. Endearing Irish accent. We both played for our school's Under-12s football team, although I cannot confirm whether George was ever made captain, as I was.

Rachel says it's that I drink too much.

I say it's because I'm dating Miss World.

Trust me, I'm Irish.

Cold Feet

TELEPHONES

Mobile phones can be very annoying things. If you are sitting on a tram early in the morning nursing one hell of a hangover as the bloody thing rattles its way to work and somebody's mobile phone rings, of course you get annoyed. If they don't answer it and the ringing just goes on and on, you get even more annoyed and you are quite likely to turn round to the rest of the people in the tram and ask the offender, politely of course, to answer their sodding phone.

When you realise that the phone is in your own coat, even though you do not own a mobile phone, you will get angry, embarrassed and paranoid in turn. When you answer it, and it is Jenny going into labour at the other end and you know you have to find Pete to get him to the hospital, then your hangover evaporates and you swing into action. Until the baby is born, a fine strapping boy called Adam, and then you set about renewing the hangover just as hard as you can.

You need to understand that all I'm doing here is saying a fond hello (or was it goodbye? It usually is) to the mother of my godson and namesake, Adam Gifford. You may think it looks more like a kiss than a greeting, and Jenny may have thought it was more like a kiss than a greeting, but Pete's my mate, for God's sake.

ADAM ON PETE AND JENNY

Pete has never been a slave to fashion. His style is as flexible as his girth. Jenny knows her mind. She also likes the last word, and for that matter, every word in between. But they are still my best friends.

THE MILLENNIUM

I'm sick of the whole thing. I just try and avoid it. Rachel and I don't have plans. We're just glad to be together. We thought we'd wait and see what parties we were invited to. What's wrong with that? I hate New Year. The Millennium is a hundred times worse. It's meaningless. It's not a moment in history. It's just a moment in time. Why do anything special?

There's no need to time the big moment, or tune into the Greenwich time signal. **Just sit outside and watch the planes crash as the Millennium Bug kicks in.**

CHILDBIRTH AND JENNY

I may not have any children of my own, but I have been at a childbirth. When Jenny gave birth to my godson, Adam. Pete was playing golf with David, so I coped in his place.

It was unbelievable, unbelievable. Nothing will prepare you for it, nothing. Jenny was brilliant. The sweat was lashing, dripping off her. She grabbed my hand at one point, for reassurance, I suppose. And then this life came out. And there it is. It's there in front of you and it was inside her and she did it all herself. I saw a whole new side to her. Well, I saw everything actually. Right there in front of me.

I feel a real man now I've lived through that.

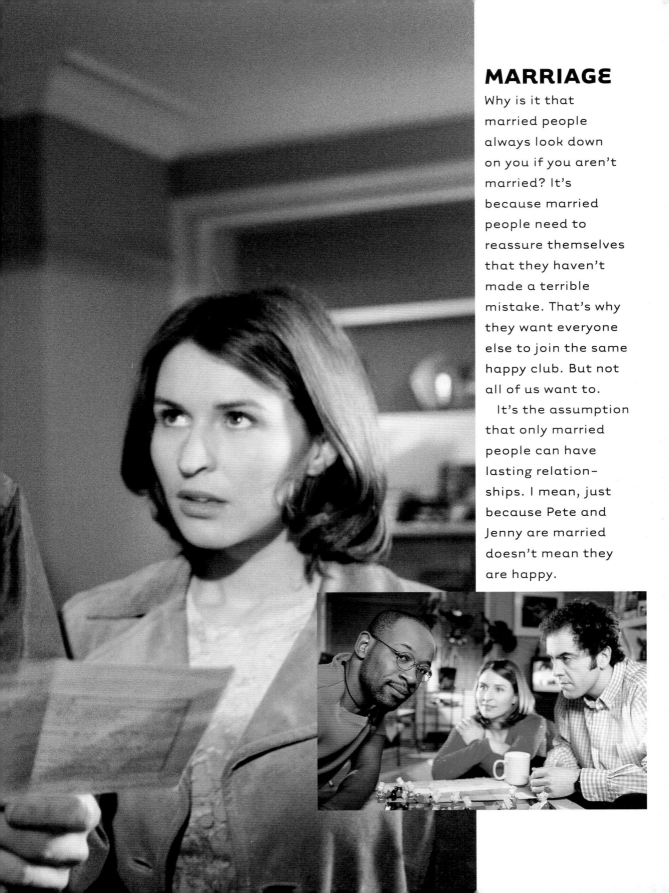

MARRIAGE

Why is it that married people always look down on you if you aren't married? It's because married people need to reassure themselves that they haven't made a terrible mistake. That's why they want everyone else to join the same happy club. But not all of us want to.

It's the assumption that only married people can have lasting relationships. I mean, just because Pete and Jenny are married doesn't mean they are happy.

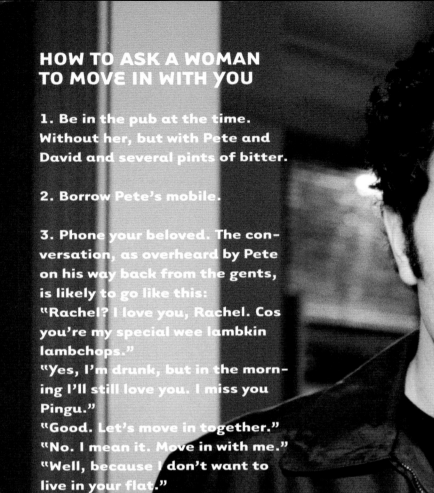

HOW TO ASK A WOMAN TO MOVE IN WITH YOU

1. Be in the pub at the time. Without her, but with Pete and David and several pints of bitter.

2. Borrow Pete's mobile.

3. Phone your beloved. The conversation, as overheard by Pete on his way back from the gents, is likely to go like this:
"Rachel? I love you, Rachel. Cos you're my special wee lambkin lambchops."
"Yes, I'm drunk, but in the morning I'll still love you. I miss you Pingu."
"Good. Let's move in together."
"No. I mean it. Move in with me."
"Well, because I don't want to live in your flat."
"Because I asked you."
"I don't care if yours is bigger. Size isn't important. As you tell me so often."
"I don't care if yours is more convenient, either."
"Or nicer! Look, do you want to live together in my flat, or not?"
"Fine. Forget it!"

4. Switch to Plan B, whatever that may be.

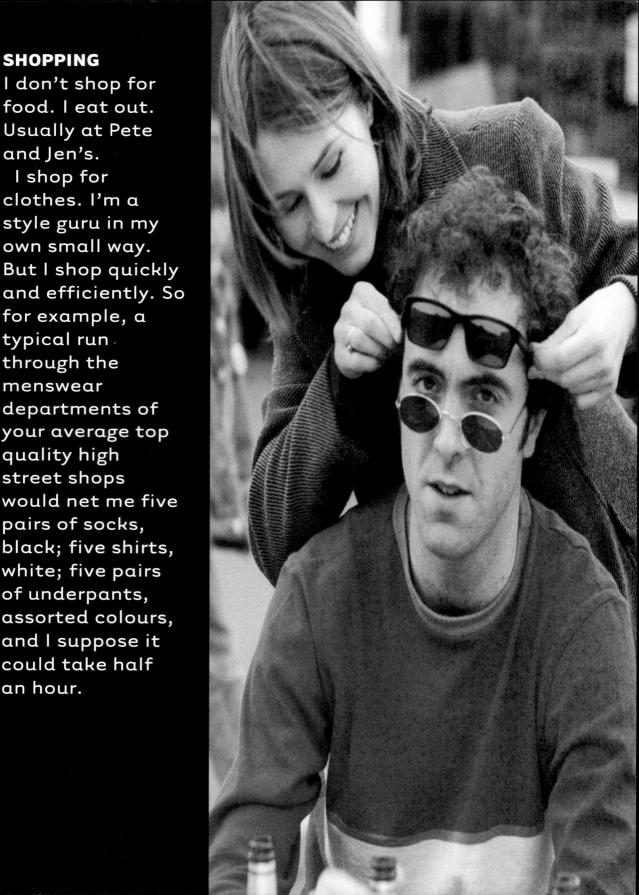

SHOPPING

I don't shop for food. I eat out. Usually at Pete and Jen's.

I shop for clothes. I'm a style guru in my own small way. But I shop quickly and efficiently. So for example, a typical run through the menswear departments of your average top quality high street shops would net me five pairs of socks, black; five shirts, white; five pairs of underpants, assorted colours, and I suppose it could take half an hour.

WORK

I'm a computer systems analyst. No point in explaining what I do,
you wouldn't understand. Suffice it to say that Bill Gates once said
(not to me personally, of course, but to somebody. Somebody who
must have been listening and who even wrote it down and told
somebody else). Anyway Bill Gates once said that if cars had
developed as fast as computers, you'd be able to buy one that did
a thousand miles to the gallon and cost $25.

ROMANCE

To look at me, you'd think I was the world expert on romance. And I am. I know how to sweep a woman off her feet and into the horizontal position.

Take Rachel, for instance. I told her I loved her by shoving a rose up my bum. Now I know what they mean when they say love hurts. Big painful thorny things, roses. I was the world's first human vase.

The rose was a bit wilted by the time I gave it to Rachel, but it's the thought that counts. Romance is not dead as long as Adam Williams is around to do the right thing.

FILMS

I love the movies. I love the popcorn. I love taking Rachel to the movies. I love arguing with her about the movies.

"What do you mean it wasn't a comedy? Of course it was a comedy!"

That's a great opening line for a debate on "The Seventh Seal" (or "Det Sjunde Inseglet" as Rachel would know it).

"Ingmar Bergman does not make comedies!" She always rises to the bait.

"Well, he should. He clearly has a talent for it." I mean, a mediaeval knight playing a game of chess with death is pure Monty Python (or Monty Python is pure Bergman – I think the Swede thought of it first). Next she'll be telling me that "King Of Comedy" isn't a comedy, either.

But my favourite film is Ridley Scott's "Blade Runner". Any film based on a novel called "Do Androids Dream Of Electric Sheep" is bound to be interesting, especially when the author is called Philip K. Dick. But add Harrison Ford, Rutger Hauer and the amazing Sean Young – a woman in a man's name – and you're sitting in front of a winner. I can't decide whether I prefer the 1982 original version or the 1992 Director's Cut, so I watch them both as often as possible.

Cold Fëët

MUSIC

I suppose my musical tastes reflect my character. A little bit arrogant, a bit of offbeat humour, always different but still immensely popular. I'm talking The Smiths here, and R.E.M. "What's The Frequency Kenneth?" could have been called "What's The Frequency Adam?" — as could "William It Was Really Nothing". Well, it'd be called "Adam It Was Really Nothing", not "What's The Frequency Adam?" but you know what I mean.

And you know when Morrissey used to sing with the Smiths with half a tree sticking out of his back pocket? *I had a rose stuck up my bum once.*

SCHOOLDAYS

I went to Sharman's Cross School, the comprehensive in Alderbrook Road, in Wythenshawe. Actually, it wasn't really a comprehensive, because there was another one on the other side of the park that took the real no-hopers. We were like a kind of grammar school.

Pete was at school with me. And old Pubes – Julian Ayres, known to all as Pubic. And Jamie Franks.

And Amanda Wagstaff. I was seriously mistaken about her. But when I was fifteen, I didn't know what a lesbian was, let alone how to chat one up. Come to that, I don't expect she knew what a lesbian was either, but she seems to have found out now.

I was captain of the Under-12s, you know. Quite a privilege, that. I was only eleven at the time. They could recognise my leadership qualities even then. And my sense of responsibility. It was a good side, the Under-12s.

I was pretty good in the classroom too. You know how they say you never for-get a good teacher? Mr. Chacksfield was the reason I went into computing. He taught me English.

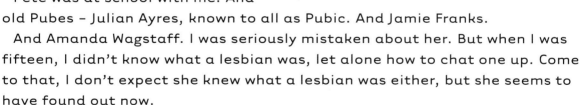

Cold Fëët

"But it's our anniversary!" I whimpered. Whimpering usually works.

"Yeah," said Rachel, ever the pragmatist. "Of the first time we had sex. Tomorrow night we can celebrate a year since the second time we had sex."

"Actually, that would be the anniversary of the third time."

Pragmatic, yes. Mathematic, no.

A couple of days later, Rachel gave me a watch to celebrate the first anniversary of the first night we didn't have sex. Black Wednesday.

ANNIVERSARIES

I hired four Mexican troubadours to play for Rachel on the evening of our anniversary. I went to a lot of trouble: Mexican troubadours are hard to come by in Manchester. I even hired a lift thing and parked it outside Rachel's office at knocking off time. It lifted us all up to Rachel's window so that we could serenade her. I even made a banner saying HAPPY ANNIVERSARY RACHEL for unfurling at the right moment. But the lift went too high, and she wasn't looking out of the window and her office is sound-proofed, so the concept didn't really work. Nor did the lift thing, which got stuck two floors above Rachel's office.

But in the end she came out into the car park.

"Surprise!" I shouted from the scissor lift on high. Actually it was more of a shock than a surprise for Rachel.

"But it's not our anniversary," she said, staring at the banner.

"Oh yes it is. A year today."

"No. Not since we first went out."

"No-oooooo." Honestly, women never remember the important things.

Later that night, Rachel said she had to go because she had a breakfast meeting in Stoke, and her only clean clothes were at her flat. I mean, what a lame excuse! Whoever heard of a breakfast meeting in Stoke? Whoever heard of intelligent life in Stoke, for that matter.

Cold Fёёt

"Hi, I'm Adam."

No. That won't do at all.

"Hello, there. Adam Williams. Remember me?"

No.

"Fancy a shag?"

How is a man supposed to introduce himself?

I suppose I ought to mention that I'm a systems analyst. If a system needs analysing, I'm your man. Systems do not get better analysis than when Adam Williams is on the job. But frankly, that does not begin to describe the real me. I'm a writer – a poet maybe – and a lover.

Rachel and I are... were... are... might be...

I've known lots of girls but there's only one Rachel. Well, actually, there's two, but we don't count Rachel Two. She went off with a bodybuilder. We met at the supermarket. Rachel and me, that is. Not Rachel Two.

In the car park. Her fault. She's always looking in the wrong direction. Still, no harm done. Just a small bump. But I thought it better if we exchanged phone numbers. For insurance purposes. I wrote mine on my card. "Adam Williams, Systems Analyst." She was impressed, of course.

She wrote hers with her finger on my rear window. Then it rained. I spent the rest of the journey home looking in the rear view mirror trying to memorise the number before it was washed away entirely. It's funny how a message written on the outside of the rear window reads correctly in the mirror. Things like "clean me" and "tosser" – you can always read them, and you usually find it doesn't rain when things like that are written on the window.

So anyway, I forgot the number. But I needn't have worried. She rang me in the end.

Thus proving the well known fact that I am irresistible.

Cold Fëët

Adam Williams

Cold Fëët

Contents

Cold Feet Programme Credits

Written by Mike Bullen
Produced by Christine Langan
Directed by Tom Hooper

Adam Williams	James Nesbitt	Zac	Chris Coghill
Rachel Bradley	Helen Baxendale	Becca	Harriet Cawley
Peter Gifford	John Thomson	Stu	John Donnelly
Jenny Gifford	Fay Ripley	Laura	Rachel Laurence
David Marsden	Robert Bathurst	Natasha	Carol Noakes
Karen Marsden	Hermione Norris	James	Richard Heap
Ramona	Jacey Salles	Nick	Stephen Moyer
Josh Marsden	Daniel and Liam O'Brien	Cabbie	Ricky Tomlinson
	Daniel and Christopher Hall	Clare	Sunetra Sarker
Baby Adam	Harry and Dean Valentine	Sally	Michelle Byatt
Natalie	Lorelei King	Doctor	Jo-anne Stockham
Amy	Rosie Cavaliero	Actor	Jethro Skinner
Noriko	Akemi Otawi	Actress	Sarah Bing
Adam's grown up daughter	Lynette Callaghan	Young David	Jordan Brownrigg
5 year old Amy	Klereese Karakoc		Tom Pinnock
Young Amy	Maddie Raven	Surgeon	Geoff Oldham
Rachel's Husband	Brett Paul	Hugh	Carl Challinor
Pete's Son	Tristan Bland	Young Pete	Peter Collins
Adam's Son	Jonathan Penney	Pete's Dad	Josh Morgan
Julie	Maggie Tagney	Javier	Javier Llamas
Professor	Brian Baines		
Rachel 2	Rachel Fielding		
Female Shop Assistant	Vinette Robinson	Co producer	David Meddick
Danny	Hugh Dancy	Associate Producer	Mike Bullen
Patrick	Sushil Chudasama	Head of Production	Susy Liddell
Terry	Ian Keith	Composer	Mark Russell
Callie	Natalie Roles	Film Editor	Tim Waddell
Muscular barman	Ryhdian Lewis		Tony Cranstoun
Stewardess	Cathy Sabberton	Director of Photography	Larry Smith
Outward bound type	Eamonn Riley		Sean Van Hales
Receptionist	Marilyn Bar-Ilan		Peter Middleton BSC
Matre D'	Ryozo Kohira		
Malcolm	John Graham Davies	Production Designer	Chris Truelove
Amanda	Jo-anne Knowles	Executive Producers	Andy Harries
Tattooist	Steve Money		Christine Langan

Cold Fëet

a man's guide to life

Jonathan Rice
Based on the scripts
by Mike Bullen

GRANADA
MEDIA